ESSENTIAL
MEDIA LAW

THE LAW FOR RADIO, PODCASTS & SOCIAL MEDIA

by Paul Chantler
and
Paul Hollins

Foreword by
HUW EDWARDS
Chief Presenter, BBC News

Liability Disclaimer

This book is not a substitute for seeking personalised professional legal advice. It should be understood that the pages of this book do not purport to offer any kind of legal advice whatsoever whether or not implied.

Laws can and do vary widely between countries and jurisdictions; you should therefore always endeavour to do your own thorough due diligence to ensure full compliance with local governing laws.

The author, publisher, distributor and any other third-party associated with this book will not be held responsible under any circumstances for any action taken in whole or in part in respect of the information contained herein.

By reading this book, you assume all risks associated with using the advice given, with a full understanding that you, solely, are responsible for anything that may occur as a result of putting this information into action in any way, and regardless of your interpretation of the advice. Therefore, this book should be considered for use as general entertainment purposes only.

Terms of Use

You are given a non-transferable, "personal use" license to this product. You cannot distribute it or share it with other individuals. It is for your own personal use only.

All copyrights and trademarks remain the sole right of their respective owner. All stories and examples shown are for illustration purposes only.

Paul Chantler would like to dedicate *Essential Media Law* to G to say thank you for the support and help over the past few years.

Paul Hollins would like to dedicate this book to his family and friends. Personal thanks go to Pam, Ian, Jake and Rumi, Simon Ross, Ian Syzling, Neil Stafford, Nick James and Ivan Laskov to say thank you for the encouragement and support

Contents

Foreword..11

Preface 13

Praise for *Keep It Legal (published in 2017)*..................................15

Chapter 1 DEFAMATION 17

The Right to a Good Name 17

We Have Free Speech in the UK, Don't We?....................................17

What Is Defamation? 17

What Is Libel?...18

What Can Be Defamatory?...19

Who Can Claim for Libel and What Has to be Proved?...................19

The Burden of Proof is on YOU!..20

Interviews and Guests..20

"Nudge Nudge, Wink Wink…"...21

How Does Libel Affect Radio and Podcasts?....................................21

How Does Libel Affect Twitter, Facebook and Blogs? 21

The First 'Twibel' Cases..22

Two More Recent 'Twibel' Cases...23

If You Can't Prove It, Don't Post It! 24

You Can't Delete Tweets..25

Bloggers Beware!..25

Beware Anonymous Posts..26

"Allegedly" Won't Protect You..26

Why 'Comedy' Is No Defence..26

Three Examples of Comedy Gone Wrong… 27

Can Repeating a Libel Get You into Trouble? 28

Can Libel Action be Taken If You're Abusive?..................................29

Is Honest Opinion Allowed? 29

Can You Libel Businesses?...30

If You Don't Name the Person, Does That Make It OK?......................30

Celebs Are Fair Game Though, Right?..31

No-One Famous Will Ever Know If I Libel Them...................................31

'Rumours' and 'Wicked Whispers' Are Risky...................................32

Take Care with Callers & Guests 33

What To Do When Your Interviewee Libels Someone 33

Beware "Creative" Radio Promos...34

Can I Get into Trouble For 'Liking' Facebook Posts?...........................35

Consequences – Costs and Saying Sorry...................................36

Should We Settle? 37

Beware – Trade Unions 37

How Do Libel Actions Usually End?..38

An Apology for Tweeting, Malaysian-Style 38

Things You Should Avoid Saying & Doing 38

Other 'Danger Words' 39

It's A Matter of Context 39

Defences to a Libel Action...39

The Defamation Act 2013...40

The Katie Hopkins Case...41

A Two-Tier System?...42

"Slapps"..42

Differences in Scotland...43

Differences in Northern Ireland...44

Appendices...45

Chapter 2 CONTEMPT OF COURT..54

What Is Contempt of Court...54

The Court System in England and Wales 54

Committals..55

Illegal versus Unlawful 56

Ensuring A Fair Trial 56

When Do Legal Proceedings Become Active?.................................56

Can I Name Someone Before They're Charged? 57

What are The Dangers of Contempt? 57

Consequences of Committing Contempt 58

Appeals 59

Inquests and Suicides 59

Three Examples of Contempt on Radio and TV 59

Court Orders 62

What Things Should You Avoid? 62

Sexual Offences... 63

'Jigsaw Identification' 63

Children, Young People and Families 63

Agency Court Reports.. 64

What About Juries and the Internet?... 64

Two Examples of Contempt on Social Media............................ 65

Why Do Newspapers 'Get Away With' Contempt? 66

The Christopher Jefferies Case.. 66

Differences in Scotland.. 67

Chapter 3 REPORTING COURTS 69

Open Justice.. 69

Attendance 69

Remote Access 70

Notes, Mobile Phone and Laptops 70

Can I Tweet from Court? 70

Court Lists... 71

Information About Criminal Cases.. 71

Information About Civil Cases... 72

Civil Hearings 72

Witness Statements and Judgements 73

Reporting Restrictions... 73

Notifying the Media... 73

Court Orders 74

TV Cameras and Microphones 74

Reporting Suicides 75

Chapter 4 PRIVACY 78

What Kind of Things are Protected by Privacy Laws? 78

What Does the Law Say About Privacy? 78

Changing Claims 79

What if Something is in the Public Interest? 79

Audio 79

Breach of Confidence 80

What's an Injunction? 80

What's a Super Injunction? 81

Are Tweeters Waging War on Super Injunctions? 81

The Ryan Giggs Case 82

The Sir Cliff Richard Case 82

Chapter 5 UK ELECTIONS 84

The Right to Vote 84

Legal Requirements and Considerations 84

Impartiality 84

Balance 85

Presenters 85

Programme Packages 85

Discussion Programmes 85

Libel 85

Phone-Ins 85

Pitfalls for Music Shows 86

Opinion Polls 86

Polling Day 86

Exit Polls 86

Chapter 6 COPYRIGHT 87

What's Copyright and What Does it Cover? 87

Who Owns Copyright? 87

How Long Does Copyright Last? 88

How's Copyright Enforced? 88

Crediting 88

Coverage 88

What's Fair Dealing? 89

What's Creative Commons? 89

Protecting Podcasts 90

Chapter 7 PODCASTS - MUSIC, BRANDING, OWNERSHIP &
RELEASES 91

Can I Use Music on my Podcasts? 91

Is Fair Use Allowed? 91

But What If I Have Permission from the Artist? 92

World Rights 92

Can I Get a Licence to Use Music? 93

Can I Just Use a Few Seconds of Music? 93

The BBC 93

What Are the Consequences of Using Commercial Music? 93

Original Music 94

Branding 94

Ownership 95

What's a Release Form and When Should I Use One? 95

About the Authors 99

Acknowledgments 101

Foreword

HUW EDWARDS

Chief Presenter, BBC News

Everyone is a publisher these days.

The exponential growth in social media platforms has created opportunities barely imaginable a decade ago. Deft operators use these platforms to great effect. The less deft risk landing themselves in deep trouble.

Making a contribution to public debate has never been easier. It follows that the room for error has grown accordingly. Social media is both a blessing and a curse. Its promotion of free speech brings with it the risk of falling foul of the law.

There has never been a better time to produce a new guide to the law applying to media activity, so Paul Chantler and Paul Hollins are to be warmly congratulated and thanked for this important guide.

Whether it's a blog or podcast or online piece or tweet or broadcast report or YouTube video - any media arena, in fact - Essential Media Law is the new reference point for all of us. It is written in a commendably accessible style; and it tackles with clarity all the major areas of media law - defamation, contempt of court, privacy, court reporting, election coverage and copyright.

Not only would I commend this work to young journalists, but I would also urge more experienced colleagues to examine its contents.

Indeed, anyone determined to make their voices heard on various media platforms would be well advised to read it carefully.

It could save you a lot of stress - and money!

Preface

Writing a book which aims to offer guidance on Media Law is always a fascinating but fraught process.

Over time, the law evolves and precedents are set – all of which makes an interesting backdrop to what you're about to discover as you make your way through *Essential Media Law*.

This book has developed over time too. It originally started as various articles and talks both of us were doing, Paul Hollins for his company's newsletter the Blue Revolution *Radio eZine* and Paul Chantler in his capacity as a consultant and Media Law & Compliance trainer for the commercial radio industry.

As we set about seeking to explain different points, we both quickly discovered that when it comes to the law, almost every aspect is connected to something else and it was tricky to explain one element without touching upon many others.

There was also a big demand in the radio industry for training, not just as a refresher for broadcast journalists but also for music presenters and DJs who - unlike their newsroom colleagues - almost always worked ad-lib without scripts and with very little legal knowledge.

So, we decided to collaborate and refine an initial draft of a few hundred words of useful notes for radio presenters into our first proper book *Hang The DJ?* in 2011 which quickly established itself as a must-read for broadcasters.

The laws covering Defamation, Contempt of Court and Privacy apply to social media, blogs and websites as well as broadcast media. Therefore in 2013 we published a new book aimed specifically at social media users called *Twibel*.

After some updates to the law, we then combined both previous books in a more detailed and definitive one called *Keep It Legal,* published in 2017.

That brings us up to date with this long-overdue new book, *Essential Media Law*. Our previous books have been considered quick-and-easy overviews of Media Law. This time we decided to expand the scope and offer a more substantive approach to include the law as it affects broadcasters, social media users, bloggers and podcasters.

There's a lot that's changed in the last few years, but the essentials remain the same. If you get on the wrong side of the law by saying something that damages someone's reputation, prevents them from having a fair trial or invades their privacy, the penalties can be eye-watering.

Many forget that this stuff is real. People can and do launch legal action against radio stations, Twitter users and podcasters. Even defending a case can cost thousands of pounds in legal fees as well as the cost of damages if you lose.

The idea of *Essential Media Law* is not about scaremongering or making you worry unnecessarily. It's simply about helping reduce the risk of finding yourself at the centre of expensive legal action.

As broadcasters ourselves, we've witnessed what can happen when things go wrong, which was the driving force in helping our fellow radio colleagues. Now we've extended that to try and help those who use social media and produce podcasts, most of whom haven't had the formal legal training offered to broadcast journalists.

In addition to the legal essentials of Defamation, Contempt of Court and Privacy, we've added new sections on Court Reporting, Election Coverage and the increasingly important issue of Copyright.

We try to illustrate the points we make with lots of real-life examples and stories.

Please note that all our content is based on the legal system of England and Wales although there's a word or two about the differences in Scotland and Northern Ireland. The detail of Libel law differs in other jurisdictions, such as the USA, so please be sure to check.

Stay safe. Keep it legal. And remember our most important advice – If in doubt, leave it out.

Paul Chantler and Paul Hollins
Summer 2022

Praise for *Keep It Legal (published in 2017)*

"A pithy, readable publication which anyone involved in broadcasting or social media publishing should read if they've not been formally trained - and a decent reminder even if they have. Written by people who know what it's like to be at the sharp end."

"For those in the media industry, the way the jargon and media laws are explained is great. Very helpful for those who come into situations like that on air, via social media."

"Anybody who is in broadcasting needs this book"

"I was already generally aware of the perils of 'publication', but this book put the flesh on the bones of my rudimentary knowledge in an interesting and highly readable format."

"A thorough refresher on media law for anyone who is currently working in or starting out in the industry."

"If you're broadcasting, this could be the most important book you ever read."

"There are lots of good books about radio, this isn't about how to make radio shows, but this has to be one that you must read FIRST. You must understand the law. I can't recommend it highly enough."

Chapter 1

DEFAMATION

The Right to a Good Name

Your parents probably taught you the old rule that if you don't have anything nice to say about someone, then you shouldn't say anything at all.

Following this advice on your broadcasts, podcasts and social media will make your mum and dad proud but also keep you out of legal trouble!

This is because everyone has a legal right to a good name.

We Have Free Speech in the UK, Don't We?

Well actually, NO.

The concept of free speech in the UK is really a myth. You can only speak or write freely after obeying certain laws made in the UK and also governed by organisations such as the European Court of Human Rights.

In the United States, it's different as there's a legal right to free speech under the First Amendment of the US Constitution. This does not exist in the UK.

What Is Defamation?

Defamation is all about ensuring the legal right to a good name.

The word Defamation literally means to "de-fame" someone. In other words, ruining their credibility or harming their reputation.

The law says everyone has a right to a good name throughout their lives, unless there's undeniable evidence to the contrary such as being convicted of a crime.

Time and society changes. What was considered defamatory 50 years ago may not be a problem today, for example calling Elton John "gay".

Defamation is divided into two parts – LIBEL and SLANDER.

- LIBEL is written Defamation in a newspaper, book, magazine, website, social media such as Twitter or Facebook

- SLANDER is spoken Defamation. Anyone making a claim for Slander must prove actual loss or damage, for example that someone has lost money or their job.

Despite broadcasting and podcasting dealing in the spoken word, anything defamatory is considered to be Libel rather than Slander because it's effectively 'published' to a large number of people through transmission.

People sometimes also take legal action for MALICIOUS FALSEHOOD. This means a statement is a lie told with malice. In other words, the person making it knew what they were saying was false and would cause harm or damage.

What Is Libel?

Libel is anything published or broadcast which "tends to":

- Expose someone to HATRED, RIDICULE, CONTEMPT or DISGRACE.
- Lead someone to be SHUNNED or AVOIDED.
- Injure someone in their BUSINESS, OFFICE, TRADE or PROFESSION.
- Lower someone in the eyes of "right-thinking members of society generally".

The use of the phrase "tends to" means claimants don't have to prove any of these things happened. The burden of proof is on you (see later).

Someone who brings a claim for Libel is called a claimant and the person defending it is a defendant.

What Can Be Defamatory?

All sorts of things can be potentially defamatory ranging from accusing someone of taking a bribe to being a liar, being a fraud or a cheat, taking illegal drugs, being a paedophile or terrorist, misusing their position for personal gain and committing a crime they didn't do.

If you falsely accuse someone of being a thief who steals money, for example, you've ruined their reputation because others may not now trust them or do business with them. They can then take legal action against you for defamation – and if you can't prove what you said, you will lose the case and a lot of money.

Who Can Claim for Libel and What Has to be Proved?

Any living individual can start a legal claim for Libel. For a Libel action to succeed against you, someone ONLY has to prove the statement you made was:

- Defamatory
- Refers to them
- Published or broadcast by you
- Did serious reputational harm

You can't defame the dead.

In England and Wales, Libel actions must be started within one year of first publication or broadcast. In Scotland, the limit used to be three years but a new law in 2021 brought it in line with the rest of the UK and it is now also one year.

Businesses, companies and organisations can also start a Libel action if they can prove serious financial loss.

Some people are easier to libel than others. For example, an Olympic legend, family man and charity worker compared to a disgraced former pop star convicted of child molestation. That's because to lower your reputation depends on how good or bad your reputation is in the first place.

People take libel action for many reasons. For example, to clear their name; to make money; to scare off other media from saying negative things about them; and because not taking action will make them look guilty.

There are also many reasons why people do NOT take libel action - the prohibitive cost (although contingency arrangements – no-win-no-fee – are available); they revel in the notoriety; they fear more could come out about them; they don't want publicity; and of course, that what was said about them is actually true.

The Burden of Proof is on YOU!

Almost uniquely in English law, the burden of proof in Libel cases lies with the broadcaster, podcaster, writer or publisher NOT the claimant.

In other words, YOU must be able to prove that what you say about them on air or on your podcast or write on your blog or social media page is actually true. The person you're talking about doesn't have to prove that you're wrong or any statement about them is false.

For example, if you described someone on a radio show, podcast or in a tweet as a "junkie" and they took legal action against you, it's up to you to prove in court that they're a habitual drug addict.

One of the most effective ways to protect yourself against the threat of Libel is to use only verifiable facts. A verifiable fact is one that's capable of being proven true or false.

So, ask yourself - Is this true? Can I prove it? Would I like this said about me?

Interviews and Guests

You're responsible for what your guests or interviewees say on the radio or on a podcast. As the producer or presenter, you're the one broadcasting or distributing the content and will therefore be held legally responsible for what it says.

If someone libels someone else on your radio station or podcast, you as the broadcaster or podcaster will be the one facing legal action.

"Nudge Nudge, Wink Wink..."

Libel is all about the meaning of words or phrases.

It also covers the following:

INNUENDO – something attributed to the words by people who have a specialist knowledge

INFERENCE – reading between the lines without any specialist knowledge

IMPLICATION – something suggested without being directly or explicitly stated

How Does Libel Affect Radio and Podcasts?

When you're on-air or putting out a podcast, you have the power to influence - and that comes with huge responsibility.

As a presenter, it's vitally important that you're aware of your legal obligations because the consequences of getting it wrong can be severe for both you and your radio station.

Although most libel cases are brought against newspapers, it doesn't mean that radio stations, presenters and podcasts are exempt.

A slip of the tongue can result in a claim for libel.

By law all UK radio stations must keep a recorded 'log' of their output for 42 days. This means if a libel comment is broadcast, then the station will have a copy of it. Chances are you'll need to provide this recording in court so an overview of context can be considered.

How Does Libel Affect Twitter, Facebook and Blogs?

Although social media may feel like a place for informal discussion, opinions and banter, you're effectively publishing or broadcasting what you say like newspapers and traditional media.

You may feel safe writing a tweet or post on your smart phone in a coffee shop, but when you press the 'send' button you're publishing what you say and the implications can have huge consequences.

Libel law protects individuals and organisations from unwarranted, mistaken or untruthful attacks on their reputation, credibility and good name.

When you post on a blog or on Twitter or Facebook, you have a REAL responsibility for what you write.

You may be able to delete your comments from your device - but your words are stored somewhere on a server and, as we'll see, you can be traced and held responsible.

You can end up being sued personally for damages and legal costs which could run into thousands of pounds.

A lack of knowledge is no defence. Saying it was just a joke is no defence. A casual, throwaway remark can result in legal action against you.

The First 'Twibel' Cases

Courtney Love

US singer Courtney Love paid more than £260,000 ($430,000) in 2011 to settle the world's first Twitter Libel – or 'Twibel' – lawsuit.

She agreed an out-of-court settlement with a fashion designer Dawn Simorangkir rather than risk going to trial over what legal papers described as a string of defamatory comments in tweets on her former Twitter account @courtneylover79.

Among other things, Ms Simorangkir was accused of being "a nasty, lying hosebag thief".

Ms Love, the widow of Nirvana frontman Kurt Cobain, argued that her rantings were merely an opinion and that Ms Simorangkir couldn't prove how they damaged her.

But the designer claimed Ms Love was influential as an entertainer and noted the power of social media to disseminate damaging comments.

Even though the case didn't go to trial, it's set a disturbing precedent in the US where freedom of speech generally trumps accusations of Libel.

Colin Elsbury

Meanwhile a former mayor of Caerphilly in South Wales made legal history when he became the first person in Britain to pay damages for Libel on Twitter.

Colin Elsbury was ordered by the High Court in Cardiff to pay £3,000 compensation after he mistakenly tweeted that political rival Eddie Talbot had to be removed by police from a polling station.

In addition to the payment of damages, Mr Elsbury was also left with a bill for legal costs of about £50,000.

He also had to publish a formal apology on his Twitter feed for damaging Mr Talbot's reputation and for causing him to suffer anger, upset and ridicule.

Two More Recent 'Twibel' Cases

A.C. Grayling

A.C. Grayling is a Professor at Oxford University and a philosopher. As part of his job, he regularly visits schools to teach Humanities.

During a Twitter argument about Brexit, Peter North tweeted, "I'd bet good money that Grayling has a hard drive full of underage botty videos". In other words, it was being suggested that Professor Grayling was a paedophile.

The tweet was seen by Mr North's 8,000 Twitter followers and was left up for eight days.

Professor Grayling took legal action for Libel against Mr North. He won the case and was awarded £20,000 in damages.

<u>Dr Christian Jessen</u>

TV presenter and medical doctor Christian Jessen tweeted false claims that Northern Ireland politician Arlene Foster, the DUP Leader, was having an extra-marital affair with her police protection officer.

Dr Jessen had 300,000 Twitter followers. The tweet received 3,500 'likes' and 500 re-tweets.

Despite requests from Ms Foster's lawyers, Dr Jessen didn't take the tweet down. It was left up for two weeks. Exacerbating the problem, he also ignored legal letters, ridiculed the legal process and didn't apologise.

When the case came to court, the judge described the tweet as "an outrageous Libel and grossly defamatory".

Ms Foster won the case and was awarded damages of £125,000 against Dr Jessen who also had to pay her legal costs of a similar amount.

If You Can't Prove It, Don't Post It!

One of the most important points is to make sure that what you write on Twitter, Facebook and your blog is 100% true.

Do NOT make claims or accusations that you can't prove in court.

Even if you think you can prove it, still be very cautious because proving things in court can be very difficult indeed.

Just because what you've said is on a website (or indeed published in a newspaper), it doesn't make it safe.

You'll have to use robust documentary evidence or first-hand corroboration from one or more people willing to testify in court.

Therefore, it's essential you make sure you get your facts right before you say what you think of an individual or organisation online.

You Can't Delete Tweets

There's a 'dustbin' or 'trash can' icon underneath every tweet sent - but clicking it doesn't mean the message is thrown on an electronic rubbish dump.

It stays briefly on Twitter's searchable index of messages and can be found for much longer on mainstream search engines, though finding specific tweets can be difficult.

All messages are preserved on Twitter's computer servers even if they're not publicly viewable.

This means that what you write on Twitter stays on Twitter forever despite your best efforts to delete. Forensic IT experts can track what down what you've written and tweeted.

Bloggers Beware!

Bloggers think that free speech allows them to write - and encourage others to write – what they like.

They can't. Libel laws apply to them and their contributors too.

Bloggers must be particularly careful if they allow comments on their blogs.

Comments can be administered in two ways on blogs – firstly, "We never moderate – all comments go up automatically", and secondly, "All comments are read and manually approved".

The latter approach gives a better quality of comment but can also bring a potential legal danger.

If a comment has been reviewed and published by the blogger and the comment in subsequently found to be Libellous, it's the BLOGGER who's responsible and not the original author of the comment.

The blogger has simply repeated a Libel.

Beware Anonymous Posts

If a blog or website fails to take down a user's anonymous defamatory post after receiving a complaint, they risk being treated as the primary publisher and sued for Libel.

The law says blogs and websites have libel protection if they act quickly to remove anonymous postings which prompt a complaint.

"Allegedly" Won't Protect You

Comedians Paul Merton and Ian Hislop have a lot to answer for when it comes to Libel.

Their use of the word "allegedly" over the years on the satirical TV quiz Have I Got News for You became a running joke – and has lulled people into believing that if they use it too, they can say what they like about anyone.

Nothing could be further from the truth.

In fact, using the word allegedly before a potentially dodgy remark about someone or something gives the clear impression you REALISE what you're about to say is dangerous.

It's perceived as admittance that you're not sure whether what you're saying is true.

Why 'Comedy' Is No Defence

Despite the wigs and gowns worn by lawyers and judges in court, the law does NOT have a sense of humour!

Have I Got News for You is the perfect example of why TV and radio comedy shows get away with not being sued for Libel.

If things are presented in a light-hearted or satirical way on a comedy show, there's far less chance of being sued than if allegations are on a news bulletin.

The key is that people must be aware of the type of show.

Many TV and radio comedy shows air comments and insults about celebrities and politicians – but it's done within the context of a well-established and well-known format which ordinary viewers and listeners are unlikely to take seriously.

Merton and Hislop have built a reputation for comedy and satire over the years. The show is also cleverly edited to give the impression that 'anything goes' and the participants can say whatever they want.

In reality, the content is screened by a professional team of lawyers ahead of transmission to ensure anything broadcast stays well within acceptable boundaries.

However, a blog, a podcast, a tweet or a radio station breakfast show doesn't necessarily have a reputation for comedy or satire like Have I Got News for You.

On radio, for example, humour sits alongside serious information such as traffic news. The law takes the view, "How could the casual listener know you're making a joke?"

When you're on-air remember that a joke or throw-away comment can easily be libellous.

Even if you make clear a comment you make is a joke, it can still get you into trouble.

Three Examples of Comedy Gone Wrong…

A highly experienced presenter on a UK local radio station read out an email from a listener inquiring about someone who used to be on air on that station some years before.

The presenter named the person and said: "He's alright. He's just come out of prison. The kiddy fiddling charges were dropped." He laughed as he quickly added, "…only joking of course!"

The radio station was sued for Libel by the person referred to - and had to settle out of court by paying several thousand pounds and the broadcast of an apology.

Many years ago, a music presenter on another radio station found himself in trouble with management when he made a joke about a famous pop star taking legal action against a publication which described him as gay and concealing his sexuality (at a time when this was considered defamatory).

As he introduced the star's song on air, the presenter said, "I can categorically say that he's not gay. He's not – but his boyfriend is." Luckily, no legal action was taken.

On a third radio station, a presenter read out a message from a listener which said that two builders working for a particular company were time wasters, slackers and always sneaking off early and for breaks. Both the workers and the company were named.

Although the presenter said on air that the message appeared to be "tongue in cheek", it still left the radio station open to potential legal action for "injuring someone in their trade, office or profession". Again, no action was taken.

Can Repeating a Libel Get You into Trouble?

YES. Simply repeating a Libel is enough for someone to take legal action against you.

In the eyes of the law, it doesn't matter if you're quoting from another source; if you repeat a Libel you're as much to blame for publishing it as the original source.

Always be VERY CAREFUL when using a newspaper or magazine story as the basis of a link on your radio show, or a blog or a tweet. Some sites are more trustworthy than others, for example the BBC website. But be careful when using sites like Wikipedia which can be amended by users.

Many people – celebrities in particular - have taken legal action over stories that were found to be untrue.

And be careful about retweeting other people's tweets. If you retweet, you are equally responsible for repeating a potentially defamatory remark.

Always exercise EXTREME CARE when using a newspaper story, social media or a website as a source.

Many radio stations use newspaper or website stories as the basis of celebrity gossip. This could repeat a story that was later found to be libellous. By repeating a Libel on air, your radio station could also be sued as well as the original source.

The breakfast show team at a radio station in the South of England once read an item from a tabloid newspaper in their 'showbiz news' slot, referring to the marital problems of a famous comedian.

The comedian in question lived in the radio station's area, heard the item – and successfully sued both the newspaper and radio station as the information was untrue.

Can Libel Action be Taken If You're Abusive?

NO. There's a distinction between defamatory statements and vulgar abuse. Libel has to be more than just an insult.

For example, you can say: "I hate Bill Bloggs. He's a tosser", that's just an insult. However, if you were to say: "I hate Bill Bloggs. He's a tosser and a liar", you'd have to prove he was a liar in court if he took Libel action against you.

Is Honest Opinion Allowed?

YES OF COURSE! The law allows people to have honestly-held opinions.

An honestly held opinion isn't libellous in itself as long as the opinion isn't malicious, derogatory or could cause harm to someone's reputation.

This means you can express strong and even spiteful views about someone as long as what you say is recognisable as a comment, based on true facts.

This means we can criticise things we see on TV, the stage and in sports without fear of legal action.

You can criticise someone's performance – but to imply they weren't trying could be libellous.

You can't go over-the-top with criticism either.

The actress Charlotte Cornwall sued tabloid newspaper the Sunday People and its columnist Nina Myskow in 1985 for commenting about a theatre performance in her 'Wally of the Week' column: "She can't sing, her bum is too big and she has the sort of stage presence that jams lavatories."

She was awarded £11,000 damages because the judge said that criticism must not "pass out of the domain of criticism itself." In other words, critics can't make derogatory statements in the guise of criticism.

Can You Libel Businesses?

YES. You can libel businesses, companies and organisations as well as individuals.

A radio station in the North-West was sued by a married couple who ran a caravan holiday business after complaints from customers were aired during a consumer feature.

During an interview on air, the presenter referred to the husband as a "con man". He sued for Libel.

During the hearing, the radio station produced 20 unhappy former customers. The company produced 20 customers who were happy. The court had to decide whether the man was habitually dishonest.

In the end, the company won £350,000 damages from the radio station.

If You Don't Name the Person, Does That Make It OK?

NO. Again, this is a popular misconception. The law states that if the person is simply identifiable then they can take legal action.

The word 'identifiable' is key as it means that even if you don't directly name the person, they can still launch legal proceedings against you if people can work out who they are from what you said or the way you described them.

If a person or group can establish that the offending words apply to them, they have a case.

It's difficult for action to be taken in the case of wide generalisations but not as things get more specific.

For example, "All estate agents are liars and cheats" is unlikely to be action-able. But if you say, "All estate agents in Blanktown High Street are liars and cheats", they're identifiable and could all take you to court.

Celebs Are Fair Game Though, Right?

WRONG. It's a mistake to think that just because someone chooses to be in the public eye that they're 'fair game' and that you can therefore say anything you like about them.

There are numerous examples of Libel pay-outs when inaccurate stories about celebrities and their private lives have been splashed over the pages of a newspaper.

Actor and singer Jimmy Nail won a Libel action against Galaxy Radio in the North-East and the Newcastle Chronicle newspaper when they described how "stroppy" he was during filming.

The radio station's breakfast show aired callers telling stories about how "difficult", "demanding" and "tight with money" he was alleged to be. He was awarded £15,000 damages.

No-One Famous Will Ever Know If I Libel Them

WRONG. It's dangerous to think along those lines because even if you work in a very small radio marketplace, streaming and digital media now means you potentially have a much wider audience, so you never know who might be listening.

31

These days it's not just your local FM or AM transmission area to which you're broadcasting.

Many famous people employ companies to monitor the media to ensure nothing defamatory or derogatory is being said or written about them. And many radio stations have 'listen again' features where broadcast programmes are archived.

It's worth remembering that the person who you've libelled (famous or not) doesn't need to have heard it with their own ears to take action. In fact, they don't even need to have heard it at the time of transmission.

Many celebrities have fans which tweet anything said by the media about them, making it easy for the stars themselves or their representatives to find out what's been said.

If they do make a legal complaint, you may be required by law to supply a recording from your own 'logger'.

The point is don't just assume that because you work in a smaller radio market that you won't be found out.

'Rumours' and 'Wicked Whispers' Are Risky

A comment can still be libellous even if it's reported as a rumour. Worse still, it can also be libellous even if it's reported as being untrue.

For example, if you were to say something like, "There's a rumour going around that Frank at the corner-shop has been selling out-of-date food, but don't worry because the stuff I've bought there has always been fine" it could still be considered libellous.

This is because the 'rumour part' is based on a defamatory comment which you are effectively repeating.

Therefore, if Frank believes that because you mentioned this rumour exists and that you're perpetuating it, he could claim that you're further damaging his name, reputation and trade and as a result, could take action against you.

If he were to do so, remember he's under no obligation to prove that he HASN'T been selling out of date food, but you may to have prove in court that he was because you repeated the libellous rumour.

Always take great care with how you approach rumours, so you don't put yourself at risk.

Take Care with Callers & Guests

On radio, if you take callers live to air or have guests in the studio or down the line, remember that something THEY say could be libellous too.

In a live situation, you're partially protected from being sued for Libel by what's called the Live Defence – otherwise known legally as Innocent Dissemination and more popularly, the "phone-in defence".

This defence says that there's a legal protection if the following factors apply:

- You were live on air
- Took all reasonable precautions to ensure a libel didn't happen
- You no reason to suspect it would happen
- You had no effective control over the speaker

Remember, though, it applies only to the guest or caller – not you or any other radio professional. You're all deemed to know better.

What To Do When Your Interviewee Libels Someone

If you're live on air and you think your interviewee's comment is libellous, you should immediately ask them to retract what they've said. Then quickly wind up the interview so they don't repeat what's been said.

It's important you don't make any mention of the potentially libellous comment and make sure you and your radio station don't appear to agree with what's been said.

Say sorry on behalf of the station (making sure you don't repeat the comment) and then move on.

If you're presenting a phone in and someone says something libellous, cut them off straightaway, distance yourself and the station from the comment and move on.

This won't mean you 'get away with' the Libel but if it does go to court, it will show that you took swift and decisive action.

Always be on your guard and keep your wits about you, even in the most innocent of circumstances.

A presenter at a local station in the South-East of England was talking to an eight-year-old competition contestant on the phone. During the chat, the presenter asked about the child's school, his favourite subjects and favourite teacher. He also asked, "Who's the worst teacher in the school?"

It was obviously meant as a bit of fun – but by asking this question, the youngster named the teacher whose reputation suffered as a result.

The teacher – financially backed by her union – threatened to sue the station. An out-of-court settlement was reached.

Beware "Creative" Radio Promos

On radio, it's not just live links that are legally risky. Pre-recorded promos and trails can also be potentially libellous.

The former managing director of a radio station threatened to take Defamation action against the new owners over the content of a promo.

During the MD's time at the station, budgets were small and the station ran competitions with a joke cash prize to match the station's frequency.

The new owners touted their big money cash contest with a promo in which an American voiceover said: "Do you remember when the boss of this station ran a competition which gave away a pound and a penny? Well, we've just sacked the guy! And now we're giving away £10,000..." The promo had aired more than 20 times.

The MD had left by mutual agreement and hadn't actually been sacked. He argued he was clearly identifiable as, though not named, he'd been the only boss of the station up till that time.

He threatened to take Libel action against the new owners for "damaging him in his trade, office or profession" (see earlier Libel definition) unless they stopped the promo being aired, apologised and paid damages. The matter was settled out of court with damages donated to charity.

In another case, a high-profile DJ on a station in the North of England threatened to take action against a smaller rival because of a promo it ran when he left. We've changed the names of the station and the DJ.

The promo, which aired multiple times over several weeks, said: "Radio ABC – the station that promised Johnny Jock a job if he ever left Radio XYZ. Well he has. And our floors have never been cleaner. Thanks Johnny".

The DJ's lawyer argued the promo "lowered him in the eyes of right-thinking members of the public generally" (see earlier Libel definition) and requested the station cease and desist playing it while reserving the right to take action for Libel and malicious falsehood.

The smaller station said they thought it was humour the DJ would have enjoyed and offered to apologise on air multiple times. The matter went no further.

Can I Get into Trouble For 'Liking' Facebook Posts?

Generally, NO. But a case in Switzerland in 2017 shows you may have to be careful in the future.

In the first case of its kind, a man who 'liked' Facebooks post accusing another man of anti-Semitism and racism was convicted of Defamation.

The posts came about during discussions on Facebook over which animal welfare groups should be allowed to take part in a large vegan street festival.

Posts describing Erwin Kessler, the president of an animal rights group, as racist, anti-Semitic or fascist, were liked by a number of people.

Mr Kessler then brought a case against the 45-year-old unnamed defendant from Zurich, arguing that by liking the posts the man spread their content by making them visible to a larger number of people, and that he acted with intent to harm and without any justifiable cause.

Zurich court judge Catherine Gerwig said at the trial that a 'like' is associated with a positive, meaning he clearly supported the posts' content. The court ruled that the defendant couldn't prove that the statements about Mr Kessler were true.

However, media lawyer Martin Steiger says the conviction shouldn't be taken to mean that from now on anyone liking posts may be at risk of being prosecuted for Defamation.

Consequences – Costs and Saying Sorry

If you have action taken against you for Libel, the legal fees and payment of damages can run into thousands – and sometimes hundreds of thousands - of pounds.

All radio stations have Defamation Insurance (usually through the Professional Indemnity part of their overall policy) which covers the costs of fees and damages. However, like home or motor insurance, the premium paid rockets if the insurance is subject to a claim so Libel can cost a station real cash.

In addition, there'll usually be a large excess. This effectively means most stations settle Libel claims directly without invoking the insurance so again, it can cost real cash.

It's possible – though unlikely – that someone suing a station for Libel might also take action against you as an individual.

As a radio presenter (whether freelance or employed), a podcaster or if you post, tweet or blog regularly, it may be worth considering a personal Professional Indemnity insurance policy which covers you in the unfortunate event of a legal case being taken against you.

Choose a reputable insurer and enquire about taking out a policy, especially if you're a radio breakfast or talk show host or podcaster. It usually costs a few hundred pounds but is worth it for the peace of mind it gives you.

The other cost to consider, apart from the ones above, is that of personal impact. Being the subject of legal action puts huge pressure on an individual financially, emotionally and professionally.

Bear in mind that if a case were to be brought against you, the radio station you currently work for may firstly fire you for bringing yourself (and/or them) into disrepute and secondly expect YOU to indemnify THEM against any costs they incur (i.e. you are responsible for any fines/damages levied against the station). Check your contract to see if this is the case (it usually is)

Any Libel action also means an increase in paperwork and meetings for your bosses as they try to sort things out with the lawyers and insurers.

In addition to damages and costs, the settlement of a Libel action usually requires an apology either read out in court or, from time to time, on air.

Apologies need careful wording so leave this to the lawyers and don't try to say sorry yourself without advice as it could get you into even more trouble.

Should We Settle?

The advice from lawyers is that sometimes it might be better to settle a defamation case out of court.

This is because there could be uncertainty about how a judge might interpret the meaning of what has been said.

There's also the difficulty of proving the truth and also huge damages and high costs could be awarded if a trial is lost.

Beware – Trade Unions

It costs a lot of money in legal fees to pursue a claim for Libel. Of course, celebrities and high earners can afford this. You might think that the high cost would put off people in ordinary jobs such as police officers, teachers, doctors, nurses and prison staff.

But the legal costs of all these workers are usually underwritten by their trade union or professional organisation as part of their membership, meaning they have deep pockets when it comes to claiming for Defamation.

How Do Libel Actions Usually End?

Defamation cases end usually conclude in one of four ways. Firstly, an apology and clarification are accepted as settlement.

Secondly, legal action begins but settlement is made involving an out-of-court compensation payment.

Thirdly, the case goes to a full trial and enormous expense.

Finally, the complainant realises they can't afford the risk of losing and simply give up.

An Apology for Tweeting, Malaysian-Style

In Malaysia, a political activist agreed to apologise multiple times on Twitter in an unusual settlement of a Libel case.

Fahmi Fadzil agreed he had defamed a magazine called Female and a publishing company, BluInc Media.

As part of the settlement, he retracted what he'd said and sent a tweet apologising 100 times over three days to make amends.

Things You Should Avoid Saying & Doing

Here are some specific things you should avoid saying about people to ensure you don't find yourself in legal trouble.

- Accusing people of a crime they haven't committed
- Alleging they're incompetent
- Alleging they're a hypocrite
- Alleging they're obnoxious
- Alleging they're negligent
- Alleging they're dishonest, immoral or a fraud
- Accusing them of sexual or financial impropriety
- Accusing them of lying
- Accusing them of doing disreputable deeds

Other 'Danger Words'

Here's also a list of 'Danger Words' - words you should be very cautious about using when talking about people as they could all lead to legal action.

This list is by no means exhaustive, but it'll give you a good idea of the types of words you should always strive to avoid:

> Adulterous, bankrupt, bribery, compulsive liar, communist, con, corrupt, coward, criminal, crook, drug addict, drug dealer, evil, fake, fraud, fascist, gold-digger, like Hitler, homosexual, hypocrite, immoral, incompetent, insane, insolvent, junkie, liar, mafia, mentally diseased, misappropriated funds, Nazi, odd-ball, paranoid, pervert, pimp, plagiarist, prostitute, racist, rapist, retarded, rip-off, satanic, scab, shyster, sleazebag, slut, snitch, spy, stupid, swindling, thieving, traitorous, unethical, unprofessional, unscrupulous, unsound, vile.

It's A Matter of Context

There are times where you need to exercise a greater level of care when making a comment or describing a person in order to avoid Libel.

As an extreme example, it's fine to describe someone as 'all fingers and thumbs' in everyday life. However, if you were using that adjective to describe a prominent neurosurgeon, then it could be deemed libellous.

This is because the description you have used is derogatory.

A neurosurgeon naturally needs a steady hand, so being described as "all fingers and thumbs" leads to a negative perception.

This could easily damage his reputation and therefore cause harm to him or her professionally.

The area of context is one where you, as broadcaster or podcaster, need to take great care. Even if what you're saying is intended as humour, the impact of your words could see you on the wrong side of law.

Defences to a Libel Action

There are five main defences to Libel:

- The Truth – (formerly called Justification). The matter is true both in substance and in fact. Remember, though, the burden of proof is on you. This means you may have to produce evidence in court in the form of witnesses and documents. If the substance is sufficiently true, a court may overlook minor details of fact.

- Honest Opinion – (formerly called Fair Comment). If the remarks are clearly statements of opinion rather than fact, then it's an acceptable defence to say that the comment was made in good faith, without malice and on a matter of public concern. This defence allows an honest person to express an opinion even if it's prejudiced or exaggerated. For example, a review of a film or theatre performance can be highly opinionated or negative without being libellous.

- Privilege - This is a complex legal defence based on public interest, which applies to parliament, court hearings and public meetings. Absolute Privilege protects what MPs say in Parliament and what anyone says in court and some public meetings. Qualified Privilege protects accurate and fair reports of those proceedings, which is why broadcasters, newspapers and websites can say what was said without action being taken against them.

- Public Interest – This is the defence that protects responsible and legitimate investigative journalism. Remember it must be something IN the public interest, not something that is just OF interest to the public.

- Live Broadcast – You're partially protected if you were live on-air, took all reasonable precautions to ensure a Libel didn't happen, had no reason to suspect it would and had no effective control over the speaker. This is informally known as the 'phone-in defence' or more formally as Innocent Dissemination.

The Defamation Act 2013

The Defamation Act 2013 aims to ensure that a fair balance is struck between the right to freedom of expression and the protection of someone's reputation.

In this legislation, there were a number of important changes to the law of Defamation:

- Raising the bar for legal action higher. This means there's a requirement for claimants to show that they've suffered SERIOUS harm or SUBSTANTIAL loss before suing for Libel (in the same way as has always existed for Slander)
- Introducing new statutory defences of Truth and Honest Opinion to replace the defences of Justification and Fair Comment.
- Introducing a defence of "responsible publication on matters of public interest" to protect investigative journalism. For a claim to be successful, a statement must cause or likely to cause "serious harm" to someone's reputation. It's also a defence that the broadcaster or publisher "reasonably believed" publication was in the public interest.
- Increasing protection for website operators that host user-generated content, providing they comply with a "take down" procedure to enable the complainant to resolve disputes directly with the author.
- Imposing general limits on those not resident in the UK taking action – so-called 'Libel tourism'.

The Act only applies in England and Wales and not in Scotland or Northern Ireland.

The Katie Hopkins Case

The "serious harm or substantial loss" test was originally thought to apply only if someone had lost their job or money as a result of being defamed.

However, in 2017 food writer and blogger Jack Monroe took Libel action against newspaper columnist and broadcaster Katie Hopkins for inferring in a tweet that she was falsely involved in or supported the desecration of war memorials.

Despite several requests, Ms Hopkins didn't retract or take down the tweet in a timely manner. The case was not settled out of court but went to a full hearing.

Awarding damages of £24,000 against Ms Hopkins, Mr Justice Warby said her words had caused Ms Monroe "serious harm to her reputation" and "real and substantial distress". Ms Hopkins also had to pay costs running into six figures.

Experts say as a result of this judgement, courts will allow robust debate online but if comments cause serious reputational harm – in other words, going 'over the top' - legal action will be upheld.

A Two-Tier System?

There are suggestions future Twitter Libel cases may be treated in a different way to those brought against broadcast or print media.

The Supreme Court dealt with the case of a woman called Nicola Stocker who claimed in a Facebook post that her former husband tried to strangle her. The court said it wasn't libellous because what she said didn't convey a threat to kill.

Interestingly and importantly, the court agreed that the meaning of words on what it called "hastily-read social media" may be different from the clinically dissected, dictionary definition of a phrase.

About social media posts, the judgement said: "The search for meaning should reflect that this is a casual medium in the nature of a conversation rather than a carefully chosen expression.

"People scroll through Facebook quickly and their reaction to posts is impressionistic and fleeting".

Some think this may lead to a two-tier system where courts in future treat Defamation cases involving social media differently and more leniently. However, right now all Defamation cases are treated the same.

"Slapps"

This acronym stands for Strategic Lawsuits Against Public Participation.

It means the way in which wealthy people exploit lengthy and expensive legal procedures – usually Defamation – to silence and intimidate journalists.

Slapps came into the spotlight with the Russian invasion of Ukraine and allegations that oligarchs close to Vladimir Putin are using litigation in UK courts to shut down criticism and deter investigations into their affairs.

A report by the Coalition Against Slapps in Europe found that more Slapps were brought in the UK than anywhere else in Europe between 2010 and 2021.

It's thought that the threat of expensive legal action sometimes leads to a "chilling" effect and discourages public interest journalism.

However, the government announced in July 2022 that new powers are to be granted to dismiss Slapps. There will be a three-stage test to tackle intimidatory lawsuits at an early stage.

The test will firstly assess if a case against journalistic activity is in the public interest, for example investigating financial misconduct by a company or individual.

Then it will examine whether there's evidence of abuse of process, such as sending a barrage of aggressive letters on a trivial matter.

Thirdly the test would consider whether the case has a realistic prospect of success.

Anyone subject to a suspected Slapp would be able to apply to the court to have it considered for early dismissal.

The government plans to legislate for this "at the earliest opportunity".

Differences in Scotland

There are some significant differences in Defamation law in Scotland.

In England and Wales, people have one year to make a claim for Defamation. In Scotland, people have three years.

Some of the language used in the Scottish legal system is different:`

- The claimant in a Defamation case in Scotland is called a "pursuer"
- The defendant in a Defamation case in Scotland is called a "defender"
- The defence that a statement is true is called "veritas"
- Evidence heard is called a "proof"
- There is a defence of "Fair Comment" which is similar to Honest Opinion

Differences in Northern Ireland

The Defamation Act 2013 doesn't apply in Northern Ireland. This means that Libel law in the province remains the same as that which existed in England and Wales prior to that date.

The threshold of serious harm or substantial loss doesn't apply and therefore a Libel action still very much relies on virtually any damage to someone's reputation.

Appendices

The McAlpine Case

This is one of the most important and high-profile Twitter Libel case in the UK to date and vividly illustrates what can happen legally when gossip on Twitter goes too far. It also shows the legal vulnerability of people tweeting and re-tweeting serious allegations.

Lord McAlpine, the former Conservative party treasurer, took legal action for Libel against broadcasters and individual tweeters in 2012.

Background

The BBC's current affairs TV programme Newsnight broadcast a report on child abuse in a North Wales care home.

The source of the story, former care home resident Steve Messham, claimed he'd been raped and sexually abused by a "leading Tory politician of the Thatcher era".

Lord McAlpine wasn't named by the BBC – but the programme led to speculation on Twitter, with him being wrongly accused of being a sex abuser. This is known as 'jigsaw identification' where small bits of information are given out and pieced together.

Mr Messham later withdrew his claims of being abused by the politician, saying it had been a case of mistaken identity.

A few days after the Newsnight report, the ITV programme This Morning featured a live interview with the Prime Minister.

Presenter Philip Schofield handed a bemused-looking David Cameron a handwritten list of names of alleged paedophiles he said he'd found on the internet.

It emerged that some of the names – including Lord McAlpine's – could briefly be seen by viewers due to the camera angle.

Lord McAlpine's Reaction

Lord McAlpine said he'd been in a state of "horrendous shock" after hearing the allegations that he was linked to child abuse.

Speaking on BBC Radio 4, he said nothing was as bad as being accused of being a paedophile.

He went on: "They are quite rightly figures of public hatred – and suddenly to find yourself a figure of public hatred, unjustifiably, is terrifying."

In the interview, Lord McAlpine said the accusation "gets into your bones, it makes you angry, and that's extremely bad for you to be angry, and it gets into your soul and you just think there is something wrong with the world."

The peer was asked about London Mayor Boris Johnson's comment that to call someone a paedophile was to "consign them to the lowest circle of hell while they're still alive".

Lord McAlpine said: "Absolutely. I think it pretty much describes what happened to me".

Lord McAlpine's solicitor, Andrew Reid, said the peer and his family had been caused "immeasurable distress which cannot be rectified."

Consequences for the Broadcasters

An allegation of paedophilia is one of the most serious slurs damaging to someone's reputation and consequently it commands Libel damages at the very top of the scale.

Lord McAlpine took Libel action against both the BBC and ITV. Both claims were swiftly settled at the High Court in London.

The BBC paid £185,000 damages and ITV paid £125,000 along with substantial legal costs. Unreserved apologies were made by both parties for the damage and distress caused.

At the BBC, the erroneous Newsnight report later partly led to the resignation of the Director General, George Entwistle.

At ITV, management took "appropriate disciplinary action" against Philip Schofield and some of the This Morning production staff.

Consequences for Tweeters

The law concerning Twitter is clear. If you defame someone via a tweet, you can be sued for Libel. Until the McAlpine case, nobody had seriously attempted to exercise that right.

Lord McAlpine's solicitor, Andrew Reid, engaged forensic information technology specialists to trace all mentions of Lord McAlpine on Twitter and other social media.

All messages are preserved on Twitter's computer servers even if they're not publicly viewable or have been deleted.

After realising they could be sued, Mr Reid said about 1,000 tweeters had written to Lord McAlpine to apologise for falsely linking him to the child abuse allegations.

They were all sent a letter saying that Lord McAlpine didn't intend to create any financial hardship for them but requesting a small donation to the BBC's Children in Need charity.

The accompanying 'Twitter Reconciliation Form' asked for home address, occupation, the number of Twitter followers, whether the offending tweet was original or a re-tweet, whether the tweet was deleted and, in the case of re-tweets, the source of the original.

It was decided that people with less than 500 followers wouldn't be pursued if they made a £25 donation to Children in Need in lieu of damages.

Sally Bercow

Around the time of the Newsnight broadcast, the outspoken wife of the then House of Commons Speaker, Sally Bercow, tweeted her 57,000 followers:

"Why is Lord McAlpine trending? *innocent face*"

Lord McAlpine's lawyers issued and served proceedings for Libel against Mrs Bercow, claiming damages of £50,000 and an apology.

Mrs Bercow defended her tweet saying it wasn't Libellous and arguing it was merely mischievous.

In the High Court, Mrs Bercow's QC, William McCormick, argued that the phrase "innocent face" was merely an indication that the tweet should be read in a deadpan manner.

But Lord McAlpine's barrister, Sir Edward Garnier QC, said only a "moron in a hurry" would have been unfamiliar with the context in which the words were tweeted.

The High Court ruled that the tweet was defamatory and Mrs Bercow agreed to make an undisclosed financial settlement to a charity of Lord McAlpine's choice.

In his judgement, Britain's most senior Libel judge, Mr Justice Tugendhat, dismissed Mrs Bercow's argument that the question she'd posed in the tweet was entirely neutral.

He reasoned that many of her followers shared an interest in current affairs and would have been up-to-date with the Newsnight story.

He ruled that her inclusion of the words "innocent face" revealed the question was "insincere and ironical".

It was therefore reasonable to infer that she meant Lord McAlpine was trending because he fitted the description of the unnamed abuser.

After the ruling, Mrs Bercow said she had learned her lesson the hard way saying the ruling should be seen as a warning to all social media users.

She said comments could sometimes be "held to be seriously defamatory, even when you do not intend them to be defamatory and do not make any express accusation."

Alan Davies

A number of other prominent people with large Twitter followings also apologised to Lord McAlpine.

Alan Davies is a comedian and panellist on BBC2's QI programme. At the time, he had almost 450,000 Twitter followers.

He tweeted: "Any clues as to who the Tory paedophile is?" He subsequently retweeted a response naming Lord McAlpine.

Mr Davies' lawyers said he didn't intend to retweet the message and he apologised.

He paid £15,000 in damages, which Lord McAlpine donated to the Royal Chelsea Hospital, and made a contribution to costs.

Lord McAlpine's lawyer, Andrew Reid, said the comedian's "reckless retweet" of a defamatory statement "fanned the work of internet trolls".

George Monbiot

Writer and newspaper columnist George Monbiot, who at the time had 58,000 followers, also implied Lord McAlpine's involvement.

Afterwards, he wrote to Lord McAlpine saying, "I'm feeling worse about this than anything else I have ever done – though I realise it is nothing by comparison to what you have gone through with the help of my stupidity and thoughtlessness."

He went on: "I helped to stoke an atmosphere of innuendo around an innocent man."

Mr Monbiot reached an unprecedented settlement with Lord McAlpine where he pledged to carry out three years of work for three charities amounting to £25,000.

Of the settlement, he said it reflected well on Lord McAlpine "who is seeking nothing for himself but wants to see work done which could be of great benefit to others".

Mr Monbiot had a cautionary word for Twitter users: "Please make sure you check your facts and think before you tweet."

<u>Lessons Learned</u>

Anyone who uses Twitter must recognise they're not taking part in a private conversation among their friends in a pub or café but that their tweets are 'broadcasts' and 'published'.

This includes repeating the words of others in a retweet. Not only can your tweets be read by your own followers but can be re-tweeted by them and read by many others around the world.

Tweets can't be deleted and remain on Twitter's servers. This means they can be retrieved by IT specialists working for lawyers who suspect Libel.

Twitter has given everyone in the world instant access to a public forum. Until recently, most people were constrained from comment by the traditional gatekeepers – journalists, broadcasters and publishers. The McAlpine case shows that this is no longer true.

Sadly, Lord McAlpine died in 2014 aged 71 at his home in Italy.

The Elon Musk Case

Elon Musk is an American technology billionaire with a net worth reported to be of about $275 billion. He has nearly 100 million Twitter followers although at the time of this case, his follower count was about 30 million.

In 2018, 12 schoolboys and their soccer coach became trapped in a network of caves in Chaing Rai in northern Thailand. The rescue team included Thai-based British cave rescue diver Vernon Unsworth.

Musk offered the rescue team a mini submarine to help but in a TV interview, Unsworth declined. Speaking of the submarine, he told Musk to "stick it where it hurts".

In reply on Twitter, Musk tweeted to his followers: "We will make one of the mini-sub/pod going all the way to Cave 5 no problemo. Sorry pedo guy, you really did ask for it".

Unsworth sued Musk in a US court for defamation and claimed damages of $145 million, saying he'd been "humiliated, shamed and dirtied" by the use of the word "pedo" suggesting he was a paedophile which he strongly denied.

Musk's lawyers argued that the word was a "playground insult" rather than a specific allegation.

They said that Twitter was a "rough-and-tumble" platform and that the site was a "social networking website infamous for invective and hyperbole".

They went on: "The reasonable reader would not have believed that Musk – without ever having met Unsworth, in the midst of a schoolyard spat on social media, and from 8,000 miles afar – was conveying that he was in possession of private knowledge".

Musk testified in court and said the word wasn't intended to be taken literally but was an insult for a "creepy old man".

The jury in the trial found in Musk's favour and he won. The case was dismissed.

Afterwards, the attorney for Unsworth, Lin Wood, said: "This verdict sends a signal – that you can make any accusation you want to, as vile as it may be and as untrue as it may be, and somebody can get away with it."

The McLibel Case

The infamous McLibel case lasted nearly ten years making it the longest-running Libel case in English history.

Two environmental activists, Helen Steel and David Morris, in 1986 handed out a few hundred copies of a six-page leaflet.

The leaflets - entitled, "What's Wrong with McDonald's: Everything they don't want you to know" – were distributed outside McDonalds on The Strand in London.

The leaflet accused the company of several malpractices including destroying rainforests to allow more grazing land for cattle used in McDonald's beef, paying low wages to staff, misleading advertising and cruelty to animals used in its products.

McDonald's took legal action for Libel and the case was heard in the High Court in London with the virtually penniless Steel and Morris conducting their own defence, having been denied Legal Aid. Detailed evidence was presented and examined.

In the end, Steel and Morris lost the case with the court finding some of the leaflet's contested claims to be defamatory and others to be true.

McDonald's was awarded damages of £40,000 but announced it didn't plan to collect the award.

The company also had to absorb hundreds of thousands of pounds in legal costs.

They justified it by suggesting that, because of the publicity surrounding the case, nobody could make the most serious of the accusations against them again unless prepared to face expensive legal action.

In 1997, a documentary film was made about the case called simply McLibel.

The Arron Banks Case

In a significant decision for public interest journalism and media freedom, the multimillionaire businessman and Brexit backer Arron Banks lost a Libel action against freelance Guardian and Observer journalist Carole Cadwalladr.

Mr Banks – who funded the pro-Brexit campaign group Leave.EU – sued Ms Cadwalladr personally over two instances where she said he was lying about his relationship with the Russian state, one in a TED talk and the other in a tweet.

During the talk – which has been viewed more than five million times – Ms Cadwalladr referred to Mr Banks and the "lies" he'd told "about his covert relationship with the Russian government".

Mr Banks claimed the comments were false and defamatory and sought damages.

After a hearing In the High Court, Mrs Justice Steyn ruled that the threshold for serious harm had been met in the TED talk but not in the tweet.

But she dismissed Mr Bank's claim concluding that, after doing significant research by reading a wide range of articles and speaking to experts, the journalist held a "reasonable belief" that her comments were in the public interest.

The Defamation Act 2013 is designed to allow for inaccuracies when journalists investigate matters of public importance.

It states: "It is a defence to an action for defamation … that the defendant reasonably believed that publishing the statement complained of was in the public interest".

The judge rejected Mr Banks's case was an attempt to censor public criticism and was not a "Slapp" (Strategic Lawsuit Against Public Participation) action.

If Mr Banks had won the case, Ms Cadwalladr faced meeting his costs – estimated at between £750,000 and £1 million – together with any resultant damages.

At the time of writing, Mr Banks has said he's likely to appeal.

Chapter 2

CONTEMPT OF COURT

What Is Contempt of Court

Contempt of Court is the law that protects the judicial process. It's separate to Defamation but equally as important.

It's wide ranging and covers things from people's behaviour in the court itself, ensuring court orders are obeyed and – relevant to us - making sure nothing is published or broadcast which might cause legal proceedings to go wrong.

The Court System in England and Wales

Our court system is complicated and – in places – confusing. This is because it's developed over hundreds of years rather than being designed from scratch.

Different types of cases are dealt with in specific courts.

- MAGISTRATES' COURTS – All criminal cases start in Magistrates' Courts. They're presided over by a bench of lay magistrates (otherwise known as Justices of the Peace or JPs) or a legally trained district judge. There are no juries. They have jurisdiction to hear and deal with minor criminal cases called Summary Cases. The more serious cases, which are called Indictable offences, are 'committed' (or sent) to the Crown Court. Magistrates can now jail someone for up to one year.

- CROWN COURTS – Crown Courts are where more serious cases are heard called Trials. Crown Courts are presided over by a Judge sitting with a Jury of 12 people, selected at random from the population. The Old Bailey is the unofficial name of London's most famous criminal court. Its official name is the Central Criminal

Court. Crown Courts also hear appeals from Magistrates' Courts.

- COUNTY COURTS – County Courts are where civil cases are heard as opposed to criminal cases. Civil cases deal with damages or compensation for a wrong done to somebody who then brings a claim to the court, for example a dispute over money owed.

- THE HIGH COURT – The High Court deals with all high value and high importance civil (non-criminal) cases. It also deals with Defamation cases.

- OTHER COURTS – Appeals from the Crown Court will go to the High Court and potentially to the COURT OF APPEAL or even the SUPREME COURT. There are also FAMILY COURTS and YOUTH COURTS.

- CORONERS' COURTS – These courts deal with Inquests. Their job is to discover the cause of death where it may have been caused by an accident or violence without established blame. Sometimes Coroners sit with juries. A Coroner records a verdict, a jury returns a verdict. The verdict could be Accident, Misadventure, Justifiable Homicide, Unlawful Killing or Suicide. If a cause can't clearly be established, the Coroner records an Open Verdict.

Committals

When Magistrates' Courts commit a person to Crown Court for trial, to avoid Contempt of Court there are only certain facts that can be reported at this stage of proceedings. These are:

- The name of the court
- Details of the defendant and witnesses
- Ages
- A summary of the charges
- The name of solicitors
- The decision of the court
- The adjournment date
- Bail arrangements – but NOT why bail was refused
- Arrangements about Legal Aid
- Whether reporting restrictions are in place

Illegal versus Unlawful

The difference between something being illegal and unlawful isn't big and many times these words are used interchangeably.

ILLEGAL means there has to be a specific law passed by local or national government that expressly makes something illegal.

UNLAWFUL means something goes against what's allowed, that is, established law but without there being a specific law to condemn it.

Ensuring A Fair Trial

One of the most important parts of the Contempt of Court law is about protecting people's right to a fair trial. The long-standing legal presumption is that someone is innocent until proved guilty.

You become guilty of Contempt of Court when you broadcast or publish material that creates a SUBSTANTIAL RISK of SERIOUS PREJUDICE to "active legal proceedings" such as an ongoing court case, regardless of your intent.

When Do Legal Proceedings Become Active?

Legal proceedings for a criminal case become active at the point of someone's ARREST, not when they've been charged.

Someone does NOT have to be charged with an offence for the matter to become legally active. From the moment someone is arrested, the case is legally "sub judice" which is the Latin for "under justice".

From that point onwards, you must be careful what you say. Never comment while a court case is in progress.

The rules no longer apply when someone is sentenced or acquitted, released after questioning without charge, the defendant is unfit to be tried or the case is discontinued.

Restrictions on what can be reported only apply in Magistrates' Courts during preliminary hearings and Crown Courts during trials as these courts sit with a Jury which could be influenced by something heard on the radio or read on social media.

Hearings in County Courts and higher courts rarely have any restrictions because they're heard before Judges only as opposed to in front of Juries. Judges are unlikely to be influenced by media reports.

Can I Name Someone Before They're Charged?

NO. In 2022, the Supreme Court ruled that anyone under criminal investigation has a reasonable expectation of privacy and now CANNOT be named by the media before being charged.

Lawyer John Oakley from Simkins, the leading media, entertainment and commercial law firm, says: "This is because a person's reputation will be adversely affected were it to become known they are under investigation, regardless of the strength of the allegations against them.

"People are presumed innocent until proven guilty but the reality is many will assume there is 'no smoke without fire'".

What are The Dangers of Contempt?

Contempt of Court can happen if a radio presenter, guest, caller or social media user passes their own judgment on a pending or current court case or broadcasts or tweets information which may prejudice jurors – like revealing a defendant's previous convictions for example.

The opinion of a radio presenter, a podcaster or tweeter (based on what he/she may have read in the paper, seen on TV or heard in news bulletins) could easily colour the view of a juror and allow the defendant to claim that they won't be able to receive a fair trial, allowing them to walk free.

Many people discuss ongoing trials in the pub or in conversation – but it's vital to understand that you can't broadcast or discuss ongoing legal proceedings on radio or on social media in the same way.

Be careful about using the phrase "helping police with their inquiries". If a person is with the police voluntarily and you identify them, you're in danger of defaming them and potentially being in Contempt of Court.

Also be careful to avoid making assumptions of guilt. When reporting a crime, for example, police have arrested "a" man not "the" man. Even some police force press releases shamefully make this mistake.

Consequences of Committing Contempt

Unlike Libel which is a CIVIL matter and settled with the award of damages and apologies, Contempt of Court is a CRIMINAL matter.

This means it carries serious penalties and punishments. You could actually be imprisoned for something you say on the radio or on a podcast or tweet or post.

If you commit contempt, a judge can issue a summons for you to appear in court and you can be arrested.

A contempt case is usually only closed once you have "purged your contempt" by sincerely apologised in open court before a judge.

The best advice here is – NEVER EVER discuss or comment on an ongoing trial or pending court case.

You should also ensure you don't comment on someone after they've been arrested or a warrant has been issued for their arrest.

And the consequences of committing contempt don't just end with you. There are much bigger considerations.

For example, your broadcast, tweets and posts could prejudice a trial and lead to a guilty person walking free. Or a re-trial might have to be arranged at a potential cost of thousands of pounds.

Unguarded words could put the life of a protected witness in danger or cause serious psychological damage to the victim of sexual assault.

Court reporting is a specialized journalistic skill and should be left to the professionals.

Appeals

There is a lower risk of contempt once an appeal has been lodged.

Although strictly speaking an appeal means a case is once again active, jurors very rarely hear appeals (unless it's a re-trial) and there's less risk of prejudicing a jury because a judge will hear it.

Inquests and Suicides

Inquests can't be prejudiced and there's no potential for Contempt in this sense. This is because an inquest isn't trying to attach any blame to an individual.

Be careful, though, when talking about suspected suicides. If a woman is found dead in her car with the engine running and a hosepipe from the exhaust fed through the window, you mustn't say it's suicide because that is for the coroner to decide. You can describe the circumstances in which the body was found and use phrases like, "Police don't suspect foul play...", "Detectives say there are no suspicious circumstances..." and "Police aren't looking for anyone else in connection with the incident."

If it appears someone has shot himself, all you can say is that the body was found "...with a shotgun lying nearby".

Three Examples of Contempt on Radio and TV

Rock FM

Two presenters at Rock FM in Preston, Mark Kaye and Jude Vause, were arrested and taken to court for something they said during the multiple murder trial of Dr Harold Shipman in 2000.

The trial had been going on a long time over several weeks. During the station's afternoon drive-time show, Mark said the following, with Jude in the background joining in:

> Mark: "I'm supposed to be delicate, but I really don't care. Harold Shipman's trial is going into its umpteeth month..."

Jude: "Guilty, guilty…"

Mark: "…It's innocent until proved guilty as sin. Put us taxpayers out of our misery because we're paying for this. Admit to it. It's a fair cop. You're caught red-handed. Be done with it"

The incident was considered particularly serious because jurors might have heard what the presenters said on their way home from the trial (which was taking place at nearby Preston Crown Court), thus potentially prejudicing the case.

It could have led to the abandonment of the trial costing taxpayers hundreds of thousands of pounds.

Trial judge Mr Justice Forbes described what had happened as "just about as irresponsible a piece of broadcasting I've ever heard."

Luckily none of the jurors had heard the broadcast. Rock FM's boss, Michelle Surrell, had to "purge contempt" by sincerely apologising to the court and the judge. Mark and Jude were given a serious reprimand by the judge but no further action was taken against them.

Shipman was convicted of 15 counts of murder and sentenced to 15 life sentences to run concurrently. He hanged himself in his cell in 2004.

Beacon FM

The breakfast team at Beacon FM, Mark Peters and Lisa Freame, found themselves in trouble when they opened the phone lines to discuss the trial of Ian Huntley in 2003. Huntley was convicted of killing two little girls in the village of Soham, Cambridgeshire.

To make matters worse, the presenters even aired their own theories about what happened and expressed their opinions on the case which was ongoing at the time. During the reporting of Huntley's evidence, they said on air:

Mark – "It's almost like the most unbelievably made up story in the world ever, really isn't it? Well I personally think it is. I can't believe that any member of the jury is going to believe that story."

Lisa – "The trouble is we don't know enough facts and we've had loads of messages in saying it may have been an accident for one of the girls but does he really expect us all to believe it was an accident for the other…. And they're saying if it was an accident, then he'd be showing some signs of remorse."

Although they subsequently left the station, neither they nor the radio station were prosecuted for Contempt of Court because the trial was taking place at the Old Bailey in London, well away from their broadcast area of Telford in Shropshire.

This means what they said was unlikely to have prejudiced the jury because they would have been unable to hear it.

Of course, these days that argument wouldn't apply as almost every radio station is streamed online via websites and apps and available to hear anywhere in the world.

GB News

During the trial of the 'Colston Four' in 2021, TV and radio broadcaster GB News was accused of prejudicing the trial after it broadcast and published opinion pieces criticising the defendants.

In commenting on the trial while it was taking place, presenter Mercy Muroki suggested Bristol council and police might have colluded with a "bunch of anarchic protesters" to tear down the statue of slave trader Edward Colston.

> Mercy - "I don't need a bunch of white hippies crippled by white guilt to throw a largely irrelevant statue in a river to prove they're not racist."

The defendants argued in court that GB News had created substantial risk of serious prejudice of proceedings. One of the defendant's lawyers said the monologue "pours scorn on the defendants and pours scorn on my client in particular".

She said the comment made during an active trial was "not only contempt, it is entirely uniformed contempt based on fundamental ignorance of what has occurred in these proceedings".

The lawyer for GB News said there'd been a breakdown in communication on the day of broadcast and that the duty lawyer only had a few minutes to look at the material while also reviewing other on-air content.

Judge Peter Blair considered whether the content constituted Contempt of Court with the risk of jurors reading or hearing it and the trial being prejudiced because they'd been influenced.

He decided not to refer GB News to the Attorney General for prosecution because of the company's swift response in seeking to remedy the position, frank acknowledgment of their errors and promises to undertake further legal training.

All four defendants in the case were subsequently found not guilty of causing criminal damage by the jury.

Court Orders

Although commenting on a case is one way you can commit Contempt, there are various other ways. These include:

- Revealing previous convictions before the end of the trial
- Identifying child witnesses
- Naming blackmail victims
- Publicising details of people under witness protection

Usually, all these things are covered by court orders which mustn't be breached.

What Things Should You Avoid?

There are many things you should avoid to make sure you don't fall foul of the Contempt of Court law.

One of the most obvious is revealing somebody's previous convictions. You should also be aware of saying someone has confessed or admitted a crime when they haven't.

Other things to watch include accusing somebody of a more serious crime, revealing prosecution evidence before a trial gets underway, making derogatory comments suggesting a motive, commenting about someone's character related to the trial, saying whether you believe someone is innocent or guilty or revealing jury deliberations.

Sexual Offences

The law gives automatic lifetime anonymity to the victims of rape, sexual offences, human trafficking or female genital mutilation. From the moment a complaint is made by them or someone else, they're classified as a sexual crime victim.

Teachers accused of committing an offence against a pupil at their school are also granted anonymity until they're charged.

The anonymity applies whether the allegation is subsequently withdrawn; whether the police have been told; or whether there's a prosecution or conviction.

The lifetime anonymity can be waived – but the victim must be over 16 years of age and give their consent in writing.

'Jigsaw Identification'

So-called 'jigsaw identification' happens when somebody who's been given anonymity is nevertheless identifiable to the public through the accumulation of details which have been broadcast or published.

Children, Young People and Families

The age of criminal responsibility is 10. This means that children under 10 can't be arrested or charged with a crime. Other punishments can be given to those under 10 who break the law.

The law stops you from including that an identifiable child under the age of 18 is involved in a criminal case or ongoing family law proceedings such as adoption or care.

Avoid naming, identifying or interviewing young people under 16 in connection with any sensitive issues. You need parental permission, preferably in writing.

Beware of going into details about family relationships, especially in the case of divorce or separation. If parents are separated and you tell only one side of the story, the other parent could challenge that version of events.

Agency Court Reports

Many court reports are sent to radio stations from news agencies, mainly writing for newspapers. Radio needs to shorten these reports for broadcast. Be careful when you do this.

- Avoid leaving out anything which affects the balance of the report.

- Make the plea clear: "Bloggs denies the charge". Make the timing clear: "The trial continues". Make the context clear: "The court was told…", "Prosecuting counsel told the jury…"

- Identify the accused accurately, not just by name. Use their age and address if available (minus the house number).

- Before writing a story from a news agency, READ the copy all the way through before writing your own shortened version.

- Be careful about organisations - such as the RSPCA, Customs & Excise, Health & Safety, local authorities - sending out press releases about court hearings. Many of them have vested interests and the information they supply could potentially be unbalanced. What they say could also be out of date.

What About Juries and the Internet?

If you're selected to be on a jury at a trial, the judge will warn you against researching the history and background online as well as tweeting, posting and blogging about the case.

This is because juries are meant to make up their mind only from the evidence that's presented in court and not be influenced by other things.

Research shows that jurors are going to the internet to look for background to cases. It may be that the principle of the sanctity of the jury room can't be maintained in the face of modern communications and social media.

Of course, jury members have always been able to go to a library to look things up or be influenced by friends and gossip with neighbours. It's just that the internet and social media make it simpler and easier.

It's important that the integrity of the jury system should be preserved and protected.

When you serve on a jury, you take an oath. When you disobey that oath or when you disobey the orders of a judge – and you're found out – you're likely to be held in Contempt of Court.

The Lord Chief Justice says a custodial sentence for a juror doing this is "virtually inevitable"

There's now a new criminal offence of juror misconduct which was created to catch jurors who researched details about a case including information about a judge, witnesses or defendant.

Two Examples of Contempt on Social Media

Ched Evans

The Welsh footballer Ched Evans was convicted of raping a 19-year-old woman in 2012.

The case generated more than 6,000 tweets with some people deciding to name the victim suggesting she was "crying rape" and "money grabbing".

Seven men and two women were fined by magistrates for breaking the law. They pleaded guilty and said they didn't realise they had broken the law by naming her - but ignorance is no defence.

James Bulger

Two men who put photos on Twitter and Facebook said to show the killers of James Bulger received nine-month jail sentences, suspended for 15 months, for being in Contempt of Court.

Neil Harkins, 35, and Dean Liddle, 28, admitted posting pictures purporting to depict the killers as adults, two days after the 20th anniversary of the murder.

Jon Venables and Robert Thompson were jailed for life for murdering the two-year-old boy in Merseyside in 1993. They were released in 2001 and given new identities.

A High Court order still prohibits the publication of any images or information claiming to identify or locate the pair, even if it's not actually them. The global ban also covers material published on the internet.

After being contacted by officials, Harkins took the post down and apologised but it had already been shared by 24,000 people. Liddle later said he hadn't realized how serious the situation was.

Why Do Newspapers 'Get Away With' Contempt?

Many broadcasters and podcasters question why some tabloid newspapers avoid prosecution for obviously ignoring the law by publishing details after someone's been arrested.

Newspapers rely on an argument known as the 'fade factor' - the gap between publication and trial which can often be up to 10 months.

They argue that the longer the gap, the less the "substantial risk of serious prejudice" of the jury.

But this is risky. Newspapers can flout the contempt laws because they act collectively, have good lawyers and big financial resources to fund any legal fights. It's not something you should do as a broadcaster, podcaster or tweeter.

The Christopher Jefferies Case

When someone is arrested and subsequently released after questioning without charge, newspapers can find themselves at risk of Libel action as well as for Contempt of Court.

Christopher Jefferies, a 65-year-old retired schoolteacher, was arrested after the murder in Bristol of one of his tenants, landscape architect Jo Yeates, 25, in 2010.

Immediately after his arrest and because of the way he looked, tabloid newspapers described him variously as "strange", "weird", "lewd", "creepy", a stalker, a peeping tom and linked him to previous paedophile and murder cases.

The headline in the Mirror was "Jo Suspect Is Peeping Tom" and in The Sun, "The Strange Mr Jefferies". In another newspaper, the headline was "Jo Landlord a Creep who Freaked Out Schoolgirls".

However, he was released after questioning and never charged. Another man, Vincent Tabak, was subsequently convicted of Jo's murder and jailed.

After consultation with lawyers, Mr Jefferies decided to take Libel action against some of the newspapers.

Not only did Mr Jefferies accept substantial damages (totalling approximately £600,000) and apologies from eight newspapers but two papers were also successfully prosecuted by the Attorney General for Contempt of Court. The Mirror had to pay £50,000 and The Sun £18,000.

Giving evidence to the Leveson Inquiry into Press Ethics in 2011, Mr Jefferies said: "In the coverage of my case, there was flagrant lawlessness. The smears were so extensive that it's true to say there will always be people who don't know me who will retain the impression that I'm some kind of very weird character indeed who is best avoided."

ITV has made an excellent two-part drama about the case called The Lost Honour of Christopher Jefferies. Actor Jason Watkins won a BAFTA award for his portrayal of Mr Jefferies.

Differences in Scotland

In Scottish courts, there's a verdict of 'Not Proven' alongside Guilty and Not Guilty. This is an expression that there was insufficient evidence, for example, "The charge was found not proven". It's an acquittal, that's the same as Not Guilty where the accused walks free.

Scottish juries have 15 members not 12 as in England and Wales. There are no opening speeches in criminal trials. The jury makes a decision based on the evidence before hearing what the advocates say.

The prosecutor in Scotland is called the "Procurator Fiscal" and judge issue a "decree" rather than a judgement.

Chapter 3

REPORTING COURTS

Most of this chapter is based on the HM Courts and Tribunal Service Reporters'
Charter newly published in 2022.

The Charter seeks to promote reporting of courts and tribunals by summarising the
rights and obligations journalists have when reporting judicial proceedings.

The media play an important role in the justice system, being the public's
eyes and ears in courts. The public have a right to attend most court hearings
but the reality is that the public learn about what goes on through news
reports.

Public confidence in the justice system and the rule of law relies on transparency
and this happens by journalists reporting court proceedings widely
and accurately.

Open Justice

The principle of open justice – that justice must be done and seen to be
done – is a fundamental focus of our legal system. Open justice is the
default position. Any qualification to it must be based on law and justified
on the facts.

The public has a right to know what happens in their courts.

Attendance

The media are entitled to attend and observe all open court and tribunal
proceedings, including those with reporting restrictions.

Remote Access

Reporters may be able to observe court hearings remotely via video or audio. Courts will try and facilitate this, but access can't be guaranteed. A timely request for remote access will help the court.

Notes, Mobile Phone and Laptops

Journalists can take notes of proceedings wherever they sit in the courtroom. Courts will normally provide designated seating. Journalists won't normally be asked to report from the public gallery.

Mobile phones and other devices such as laptops can be used by the media in the courtroom as long as they don't disturb court users.

Can I Tweet from Court?

Video and audio recording has long been barred from courts. In general, that applies to tweeting and texting too.

Members of the public are NOT allowed to tweet or text from court without permission.

The former Lord Chief Justice, Lord Judge, says the danger of tweeting is likely to be most acute during criminal trials.

"Witnesses who are out of court may be informed of what has already happened in court and so coached or briefed before they then give evidence," he said.

In addition, ordinary people in the public gallery could hear information that the jury may have been prevented from hearing, for example the identity of a rape victim. But this can't be reported.

Therefore, the danger of a trial being seriously prejudiced or impeded is obvious.

However, the guidance says bona fide journalists ARE allowed to tweet without permission because they understand the rules and don't pose a danger of interference to the proper administration of justice.

Unlike the public, reporters don't need to ask permission to report in this way. The judge or magistrate does however retain discretion to prohibit this if necessary.

Explaining why journalists should be treated differently from the public, Lord Judge said: "The difference is that John and Jane Citizen are less likely to understand the rules of contempt than most journalists who come into my court."

Journalist tweets should relate to FACTUAL matters only, such as what's said in court by witnesses, lawyers or judges.

Tweets mustn't contain COMMENT such as, "The witness is buckling under cross examination" or "The jury doesn't seem impressed by this evidence".

Court Lists

Court lists are available to all, free of charge, and should normally be online or in hard copy in the court building by the morning a hearing is listed.

In criminal cases, at a minimum, the media court lists should contain the time and place of the hearing, the defendant's name, age, address, and where known, their occupation and the alleged offence.

In civil cases, the list should contain the time and place of the hearing, the names of the parties, the judge and the courtroom. Providing such information doesn't breach data protection legislation.

Information About Criminal Cases

The law says journalists are entitled to the following information if the case is ongoing, unless (exceptionally) the information is prohibited by a reporting restriction:

- Date of any public hearing
- The alleged offence and plea entered
- The court's decision and any decision about bail or committal
- Whether the case is under appeal
- The outcome of the case and any appeal
- The identity of the prosecutor, the defendant (including their date of birth), the parties' representatives and their addresses, and the judge or magistrates
- Any reporting restrictions

Copies of the charge sheet or indictment should be provided to the media on request.

Information About Civil Cases

Once civil proceedings have started, the fact of the claim can be made public including the name of the parties and legal representatives. Anyone can obtain from court records a copy of a statement of case (but not any documents attached) and a judgement or order given.

Permission isn't needed from the court and the parties don't need to be notified. The court can order that disclosure not take place and an application can be made for access to other documents on the court file. A fee may be payable.

Civil Hearings

To understand proceedings and support the principle of open justice, access should normally be allowed to the documents in civil cases, including witness statements in open court.

Reporting proceedings without access to documents can become impossible given a significant amount of the argument and evidence is in written form.

While there's no automatic right of access to court records that weren't read in open court, case law encourages disclosure of documents when it advances the principle of open justice.

Witness Statements and Judgements

A witness statement which stands as evidence is open to inspection during the course of a trial unless the court directs otherwise.

Journalists can be given judgements or orders made, whether they've been made at a hearing or without a hearing

Reporting Restrictions

Journalists can report what happens in open court proceedings, subject to any court order. Information about a case or hearing can still be given to the media even when reporting restrictions apply.

It's the media's responsibility to ensure that what's broadcast or published complies with the law. The decision on what to broadcast or publish rests with the media.

Notifying the Media

A party seeking a reporting restriction must apply to court and notify and other party or person as the court directs.

The media should be notified of a reporting restriction application and given an opportunity to make representations. Court orders restricting reporting should be considered at a pre-trial or pre-inquest stage and may be considered in advance.

If the application is for the trial to be held in private, court staff should display a notice of the application at a prominent location near the courtroom and notify the media.

If the media wish to oppose the application for a reporting restriction, they can make representations to the court either in writing or orally.

Court Orders

Any order restricting reporting should be put in writing as soon as possible and the media made aware of the order on the court register.

Breach of an order imposes potential criminal liability, so it's vital the terms of the order are clear, in writing and made known.

The order should set out the date, name of the trial, who made the order, the reason for the order, its legal basis, who's affected by the order and how long it lasts. Orders that are rescinding, replacing, updating or amending previous orders must make this clear.

Once an order is made, court staff should display a notice by the courtroom door, on the daily lists or court register or any room available for journalists.

At the beginning of a hearing, the judge should inform those present (in person or remotely) if there's a reporting restriction in place. However, the responsibility of finding this out remains with reporters.

TV Cameras and Microphones

In summer 2022 as this book was being published, TV cameras and microphones were allowed into criminal trials for the first time. This is a major change in the law.

Coverage will be restricted to the judge handing down a sentence and explaining the reasons for it, with a time delay to avoid broadcasting any violent or abusive reaction.

Viewers will get to see inside the courtroom for about half an hour but the cameras will be fixed firmly on the judge with no view of the defendant, victims, jurors, lawyers or witnesses.

Only Crown Court proceedings will be televised. Broadcasting of entire trials will remain prohibited, unlike in some other countries.

Each sentencing that is filmed will be uploaded to YouTube so viewers can see the judge's full reasoning and his or her explanation of the law.

Lord Chief Justice Lord Burnett said: "It is an exciting development because it will help the public to understand how and why criminals get the sentences that they do.

"Open justice is important and the sentencing of serious criminal cases is something in which there is legitimate public interest.

"It has always seemed to me that this is part of the criminal process that can be recorded and broadcast in many cases, but not all, without compromising the administration of justice or in the interests of justice."

Photography was banned in all UK criminal courts after the publication of a 'snatched' photo of notorious wife killer Dr Crippen standing in the Old Bailey in 1910.

The introduction of cameras and microphones follows a long campaign by major broadcast news organisations, the BBC, ITN and Sky.

Cameras were allowed first into the Supreme Court in 2009 and then the Court of Appeal four years later.

The judiciary have opposed court cameras for a long time, worried that they would show the stress of the victims and witnesses and encourage lawyers to show off.

Cameras were allowed into Scottish courts in 1992 and are permitted in courts all over the world to varying degrees.

Reporting Suicides

The Samaritans charity in the UK publishes a ten-point list of guidance for when the media reports suicides:

1. Avoid reporting methods of suicide, such as describing someone as having died by hanging

2. Include references to suicide being preventable and signpost sources of support, such as Samaritans' helpline. This can encourage people to seek help, which could save lives – "When life is difficult, Samaritans are here – day or night, 365 days a year. You can call them for free on 116 123, email them at

jo@samaritans.org, or visit www.samaritans.org to find your nearest branch".

3. Avoid dramatic headlines and strong terms such as 'suicide epidemic'. Never suggest that someone died instantly or that their death was quick, easy, painless, inevitable or a solution to their problems. Steer clear of language that sensationalises or glorifies suicide.

4. Don't refer to a specific site or location as popular or known for suicides, for example, 'notorious site' or 'hot spot' and refrain from providing information, such as the height of a bridge or cliff.

5. Avoid dramatic, emotive or sensational pictures or video footage. Excessive imagery can glamourise a death and lead vulnerable individuals to over-identify with the deceased.

6. Avoid excessive amounts of coverage and overly prominent placement of stories and don't link to previous stories about suicide.

7. Treat social media with particular caution and avoid mentioning or linking to comments, or websites/forums that promote or glamourise suicide. Similarly, it's safer not to open comments sections on suicide stories and careful consideration should be given around the appropriateness of promoting stories through push notifications.

8. Including content from suicide notes or similar messages left by a person who has died should be avoided. They can increase the likelihood of people identifying with the deceased. It may also romanticise a suicide or cause distress to the bereaved family and friends.

9. Speculation about the 'trigger' or cause of a suicide can oversimplify the issue and should be avoided. Suicide is extremely complex and most of the time there's no single event or factor that leads someone to take their own life.

10. Young people are more susceptible to suicide contagion. When covering the death of a young person, don't give undue prominence to the story. Don't use emotive, romanticised language or images – a sensitive, factual approach is much safer. Coverage that reflects the wider issues around suicide, including that it's prevent-

able, can help reduce the risk of suicidal behaviour. Include clear and direct references to resources and support organisations.

Chapter 4

PRIVACY

What Kind of Things are Protected by Privacy Laws?

There are different types of information which could infringe an individual's privacy.

This includes putting into broadcasts or podcasts secret recordings made without permission or information from leaked documents. You should also be careful of including information about medical conditions, treatments and details of an individual's health generally.

Personal financial matters would also be considered private as well as family breakdowns including child custody and issues of sexuality and gender identity.

What Does the Law Say About Privacy?

UK Privacy Law stems from Human Rights legislation together with case law established over many years in courts.

It seeks to balance an individual's right to privacy with the media's right to freedom of expression.

This balancing act starts with questioning whether an individual has a reasonable expectation of privacy.

If they can expect privacy, do we have a right to firstly record any audio of them and secondly include it in a broadcast or podcast?

If we don't have their consent, the judgement is whether it's warranted to record audio and include it. By warranted, we need to decide whether it's justified in the circumstances or in the public interest.

Changing Claims

In the last few years, there's been a shift towards legal claims for privacy as opposed to claims for Defamation, particularly among celebrities.

The attraction is that, unlike Defamation, privacy laws stamp out negative – but possibly true - stories before they appear. High profile individuals use privacy laws rather than Libel laws to control their media profile.

Privacy action has become increasingly fashionable as it can stop potentially damaging articles from seeing the light of day. Libel laws just set the record straight.

In a practical sense, privacy claims are much easier for claimants to make as there's no threshold for harm, as in a Defamation case, and no time limits to make a claim

What if Something is in the Public Interest?

There are some forms of content that can be justified as being in the public interest.

These include stories which expose false or misleading claims made by individuals, businesses or organisations; stories which protect public health or safety; stories which help with the detection of crime; and stories which expose wrongdoing, maladministration or incompetence that affects the public.

Remember being IN the public interest isn't the same as being OF interest to the public.

Audio

The use of audio recordings of someone talking about a sensitive situation in broadcasts or podcasts could be subject to legal action for breach of privacy. Usually, you'll need to obtain permission from someone both to record and include audio featuring them.

Essentially, people must give informed consent for their inclusion. Informed consent means they should know that their contribution will be used and in what context.

If you don't have their consent (it's best to record this before or after the interview), you must ask yourself whether the inclusion of it is justified in the public interest.

If you lack the public interest justification, you may still be able to use the audio if you protect identification of the individual – for example, you could anonymise or disguise it by using a false name, having it voiced by an actor or altered technically to change the voice featured.

Unless you do this, you're at risk of breaching privacy laws.

Breach of Confidence

Legal action can be taken where sensitive or confidential information has been leaked. The information must have been given in circumstances where there's an expectation of confidence, for example between an employer and an employee. There must also have been an unauthorised use of that information to the detriment of the individual or organisation that created the material.

A claimant can seek damages and costs if the material has already been published or, if not, seek a legal injunction to stop the information from being made public

What's an Injunction?

An Injunction is a court order which prevents the publication of certain details of a legal case including identities or actions.

Injunctions – sometimes known in the press as 'gagging orders' - were originally created to protect people whose lives might be at risk if their details were made public, such as child sex offenders.

However, with the passing of the Human Rights Act 1998, judges began to extend the powers of injunctions. Entertainers, sports stars, actors and many more have used injunctions to protect their privacy if they find out something sensitive or embarrassing is about to be broadcast or published about them.

Injunctions can also be used to stop broadcast or publication of other things, such as news stories based on documents which can be shown to have been stolen.

What's a Super Injunction?

A Super Injunction is a powerful legal order which not only prevents the media from reporting the details of a story covered by an injunction but also forbids mention of the very existence of the injunction itself.

If you ignore injunctions or report the existence of super injunctions, you could be found guilty of Contempt of Court and sued for invasion of privacy, while those making false accusations could be sued for Libel.

Super Injunctions are very rarely granted – and if they are, only for short periods of time. More common is the Anonymised Injunction where not only is something stopped legally but the names of either or both parties to the proceedings aren't revealed.

Users ignoring injunctions or reporting the existence of super injunctions could be found guilty of Contempt of Court and sued for invasion of privacy, while those making false accusations could be sued for Libel.

Are Tweeters Waging War on Super Injunctions?

Twitter has found itself at the centre of the debate about Super Injunctions.

While newspapers, broadcasters and other traditional mainstream media are being restricted in what they can report, thousands of Twitter users have posted tweets and re-tweets circulating information covered by injunctions and super-injunctions.

Are these tweeters beyond the reach of the law?

In practice, legal experts expect tweeters to find safety in numbers if enough defy an injunction simultaneously.

It's not the letter of the law that protects tweeters, but the sheer difficulty of singling out and tracking down so many offenders.

Esteemed legal analyst and broadcaster Joshua Rozenberg says: "Clearly, they are at risk, but if there are a lot of them there's little chance of them being prosecuted… although if there was one individual who could be seen to have instigated the whole thing, that would be very different."

The Ryan Giggs Case

Professional footballer Ryan Giggs obtained an injunction in 2011 to prevent publication of details of an alleged affair with reality TV star Imogen Thomas.

Newspapers and broadcasters were initially unable to name Giggs or even refer to the existence of an injunction.

However, a tweeter revealed Giggs' identity. Public interest was such that the record for visits to Twitter at the time was exceeded.

The allegations were repeatedly retweeted by 75,000 people, making it difficult to take legal action against any one individual. The judge declined to renew Giggs' injunction. No action was taken against the tweeters.

Nevertheless, legal action was instigated by Giggs against Twitter itself in an attempt to obtain information about which tweeters were involved.

Ironically, this then led to the footballer's name and the allegations being repeated many more times across social media and, as a consequence, by the mainstream media.

The Sir Cliff Richard Case

One of the most famous cases of legal action for invasion of privacy relates to singer and musician Sir Cliff Richard.

As a result of a historical allegation of the sexual assault of a child at an Evangelical rally in Sheffield, police raided Sir Cliff's apartment in Sunningdale, Berkshire, in 2014.

The BBC were tipped off about the raid and not only named Sir Cliff and reported from outside the grounds of the gated community but also filmed the search from a helicopter, including shots zooming in on police through the windows of the apartment while they conducted their search.

Sir Cliff strongly denied the allegations which he said were "absurd and untrue". He was neither arrested nor charged with any offence. In fact, he was at his home in Portugal watching the raid live on TV.

Ten months later, the Crown Prosecution Service said there was insufficient evidence for any case to proceed and no further action would be taken.

Sir Cliff sued both the police and the BBC for invasion of privacy. South Yorkshire Police settled out of court for £400,000. The BBC defended itself in court but lost the case and were ordered to pay £210,000 damages. The BBC's estimated legal fees were £1.8 million and they had to pay Sir Cliff's legal costs too which were £2 million.

The judge, Mr Justice Mann, said the BBC had infringed Sir Cliff's privacy in a "serious and sensationalist way" and the use of a helicopter to film the police raid on his home was "excessive and disproportionate".

Now Sir Cliff has joined a pressure group pushing for anonymity for those accused of sexual offences.

Chapter 5

UK ELECTIONS

The Right to Vote

Reporting restrictions on General and Local Elections only apply to BROADCASTERS. Podcasts and social media can say what they wish if it doesn't fall foul of Libel laws.

The Law takes a stern view of any broadcaster who prejudices the FAIR-NESS of a General Election. Political parties monitor stations for any hint of bias.

The Election Period starts with the Dissolution of Parliament. After this date the rules come into effect. This usually coincides with the announcement of Polling Day.

Legal Requirements and Considerations

The aim is to achieve BALANCE of coverage of each party over the campaign as a whole. The media regulator, Ofcom, say broadcasters should use their own judgement of parties based on evidence of past and current electoral support. Ofcom usually publishes a digest of this to help and it's available via the Ofcom website.

Impartiality

There's no requirement to give equal time to all parties. Not every party has to feature in every item. But overall coverage must be IMPARTIAL across the campaign. In other words, you must be seen not to be supporting any one side and all major parties must be treated equally.

Balance

To achieve balance, news teams would be wise to keep timing sheets over the length of the campaign recording the coverage given, duration, in what form (copy, interview, wrap/package) and transmission time.

Presenters

Candidates mustn't act as presenters during the Election Period. Presenters must also remain neutral. Several radio stations have been fined by Ofcom after presenters declared their political allegiance on air.

Programme Packages

Constituency reports must include equal contributions from each of the main parties. On first broadcast the same day, the package must include the name and party of every candidate. Subsequently, you can direct listeners to a website link.

Discussion Programmes

All candidates must get roughly equal airtime. A stopwatch isn't needed but there must be no glaring discrepancy. The chair must be impartial but put forward policies of absent candidates for discussion.

Libel

Beware candidates saying something defamatory during discussions, particularly accusations of racism, fascism and lying. It's no defence to say you are simply reporting what someone else said. However, if you're reporting a public meeting, you're protected from Libel by the defence of Privilege (see earlier) if the report is accurate, fair and without malice.

Phone-Ins

Candidates shouldn't appear on phone-ins as callers (either election or general programmes) as it could cause problems with balance. You should ask each caller off air whether they're standing in the election. A range of views should be reflected. Presenters shouldn't take advantage of their position on air. Where alternative views aren't available, presenters should summarise an alternative point of view.

Pitfalls for Music Shows

Presenters should avoid flippant comments, reactions after news bulletins, comedy promos and any reference to politics.

Opinion Polls

Polls can be reported as news as long as the terminology is correct. Polls "suggest", they don't "show" or "prove".

Polling Day

Polls open at 7am and close at 10pm on Polling Day. During this time, NO political comment must be broadcast at all, even if it's balanced. Basic facts are allowed – the weather, general predictions about turnout, politicians voting – but NOTHING ELSE. From 10pm, all restrictions end.

Exit Polls

It's unlawful to publish the results of an exit poll before polling has finished.

Chapter 6

COPYRIGHT

What's Copyright and What Does it Cover?

A judge once said that "anything worth copying is worth protecting" – and that's the essence of Copyright Law. It's a complicated legal area so be careful before using material protected by copyright.

Copyright Law is important for podcasters in two specific ways – what you can use on your podcasts and for preventing others from stealing your podcast content.

Copyright protects intellectual property - the products of people's creativity, skill, labour or time. The product must be original with work or effort having gone into creating it. And it needs to be substantial too. Things like single or pairs of words, brief slogans and catchphrases are ruled to be too trivial to protect.

Copyright also protects the tangible expression of ideas. This means if someone takes their idea of for a podcast and records it, then that expression – in other words, the recording - is protected under a copyright.

The same is true if you want to use material from a book, a film, lyrics from a song and other creative works.

Who Owns Copyright?

The law rewards creativity by protecting it and once you are the copyright holder and owner, you have the exclusive right to use the original work.

The first owner of the copyright is the creator or author. If the creator is employed by someone, the owner will be the employer. If the creator is a freelancer or contractor working for someone else, they'll own the copyright unless otherwise stated.

In films, television and sound (including podcasts), the copyright owner is the person or organisation that arranged for the recording or film to be made such as the podcaster, producer or production company.

It's a general guide that if you don't own the copyright, then someone else does.

How Long Does Copyright Last?

Copyright lasts for the lifetime of the creator or author and then a further 70 years.

How's Copyright Enforced?

Copyright is more rigorously enforced these days than it used to be because of the way that the internet makes material available to a wide number of people. People are increasingly aware of the ownership of their intellectual property and will say they want at least a credit for any use if not a payment.

If you use someone else's content without consent or agreement, you can expect to receive an invoice for its use.

Crediting

The best general advice is to always CREDIT the copyright owner. If you wish to use third party content, you must either - obtain written consent; credit the copyright owner; or possibly pay for the usage.

Coverage

Copyright covers work that is 'fixed' – in other words, it must be written, recorded, filmed, photographed or stored on a computer.

Copyright applies automatically and doesn't need to be registered. There's no copyright on news, facts, ideas or information.

In other words, if you want to do a true crime podcast, the idea of that podcast isn't protected. However. if you record a specific podcast about a true crime, the particular content within that episode is protected by copyright. Other podcasters can't create that episode word for word or use audio from your podcast without permission from you, the creator.

Copyright applies to written material, books and articles, music and audio, films, radio and TV, magazine and newspaper design, databases, photos, logos, graphics and of course podcast content.

What's Fair Dealing?

Fair dealing allows you to use a reasonable - or even substantial - amount of copyrighted material provided the copyright owner is given credit. It even allows use when the copyright owner has refused consent. There's no specific guide about what is reasonable or substantial; it's simply a judgement.

There are various types of fair dealing: for the purpose of reporting current events; for the purpose of criticism or review; for the purpose of caricature or parody; and for the use of a quotation from a copyright work. For example, a film podcast reviewing new releases might use an audio clip to criticise, even though the film producer owns the copyright. That's allowed under fair use.

There are no hard-and-fast rules about what constitutes fair dealing but in general you should ask yourself whether the use of copyright material is to comment, criticise or to use for comedy value. If so, you have a chance of using fair dealing as a defence to any copyright claim.

What's Creative Commons?

On many digital platforms, such as YouTube, users can offer Creative Commons licences in relation to copyright works. This states that the content can be used with a credit to the owner. Some Creative Commons licences restrict the use of material for commercial purposes or to restrict editing. The small print of these licence conditions is important to check and respect.

Protecting Podcasts

Obtaining copyright protection for your podcast is simple. The two requirements that must be met are that the podcast must firstly be original and secondly that it's fixed in a tangible means of expression.

Originality is straightforward. A podcast is original if it was created independently and made with a certain amount of creativity. This means it was not copied from something else.

It doesn't have to be an original idea as ideas aren't protected but it must be an original expression of an idea. There must also be some creativity involved.

Only a small element of creativity is needed as this is a low barrier to meet. Essentially it means that some creative decision making must have gone into the podcast.

A well-known and quoted example is that of an old-style phone book. If you were to read the phone book on a podcast you wouldn't be protected. However, reading information from the phone book in a different order would be protected!

The fixation requirement transforms an original idea into a legally protected copyright work. In a podcast context, this means the recording. It doesn't have to be online or available to be protected; recording is a tangible fixed means of expression in itself.

Chapter 7

PODCASTS - MUSIC, BRANDING, OWNERSHIP & RELEASES

Information for this chapter was based on an article How to Use Commercial Music in Your Podcast written in 2018 and updated in 2020. We are grateful to the author JAMES CRIDLAND, who also produces the excellent and highly recommended daily newsletter for the podcasting industry, Podnews.net.

Can I Use Music on my Podcasts?

There are a lot of myths and misinformation about the use of commercial music in podcasts. The only correct answer is – NO, you can't use commercial music in your podcast.

It doesn't matter whether your podcast makes money. Unfortunately, you don't have the right to use any commercial music.

The music business has many appetites to satisfy. When a songwriter writes a song, they've created a work of authorship so there's copyright in the composition. These compositions are managed by a music publishing company which has essentially bought the song from the writer in exchange for paying them a percentage of the revenue. When the song is recorded by a recording artist, there's a second part of creative work – the recording. This is usually owned by the record company that paid for and is distributing the recording.

So, when you're using a piece of recorded music, you can't just use it because it's available. You must obtain permission which covers both the composition and the recording.

Is Fair Use Allowed?

There's no standard for fair use of commercial music in podcasts. Fair use or fair dealing is different across the world.

The law which is relevant is copyright law in countries where the material is *available* not *hosted* or *produced*. For example, French copyright law applies to anything published or performed in France, regardless of where it was originally created.

Fair use is also defence you use in court which is normally decided on a case-by-case basis. It's up to you to prove that your use was fair and not an infringement. If you've already ended up in court, you've probably spent a lot of money in legal costs irrespective of whether you have a right under fair use.

In short, fair use is a dangerous defence on which to rely.

But What If I Have Permission from the Artist?

Having the permission of the artist doesn't allow you to use commercial music in your podcast. The artist is just one part of the equation: you also need permission from the record company, the composer and the publishers of the music. In many cases you'll also need to have the right (called "mechanical" or "sync") which allows you to copy the music onto your podcast.

In most cases, the artist can't grant permission because they signed a contract with music publishers and record companies.

The RIAA who work for US record companies have shut down podcasts which claimed to have the permission of the artists. It's just not enough.

World Rights

Even if you live in the US and your use of music is acceptable under US law, it's not acceptable to use everywhere. The rest of the world doesn't follow US law. And the law that matters for copyright purposes is the law where the podcast is *consumed*.

It's technically possible to ensure that the podcast isn't available anywhere other than the US via what is called "geo-locking". Big broadcasters such as the BBC and NPR and some other podcast producers do this on some platforms. Other companies that do this include the TV streaming service Netflix.

Can I Get a Licence to Use Music?

Some countries offer licences which purport to allow you to use music in your podcast, such as PRS for Music in the UK. However, beware. Ensure that any licence covers everything you need including the use of the recording.

Many licences include lots of caveats. Anchor/Spotify have announced Shows with Music which is a way to put full tracks into your podcasts. Welcome though this is, restrictions include that you can only hear these podcasts on Spotify not on any other platform, listeners can only hear the songs in full if they pay for Spotify Premium and there are rules about how much talk you're allowed and where ads go.

Can I Just Use a Few Seconds of Music?

There's no minimum duration where it's acceptable to use commercial music in a podcast. Any suggestion of "you're allowed to use 30 seconds" is just misinformation.

The BBC

Big broadcasters like the BBC spend millions on their music licensing. Some publishers managed to negotiate some use of short clips of commercial music for podcasts as part of their overall music licences. This use is unavailable to anyone not already spending millions on music in the first place.

What Are the Consequences of Using Commercial Music?

You can face legal action for using commercial music in your podcast. Some podcasters have been taken off platforms for using music without permission.

There's a company called Pex which automatically scans podcasts for unauthorised music use. The company is already successfully being used on social media. It's similar to technology by photographic agency companies such as Getty Images to identify and take action against people using unauthorised images on websites.

In terms of legal action, the reality is that record companies and copyright holders are unlikely to prosecute if it's not worthwhile for them as it costs them money in legal fees. There are lots of reasons why they might make an example of a high-profile podcaster - but also reasons why they might choose to look the other way.

The gamble is that record companies may well just sit and wait for you to become successful and then come after you, maybe in two years when you can afford it.

In short, if you go ahead with it anyway you might just get away with it for a while. But the bots are coming and that is unlikely to be a good plan for long.

Original Music

Of course, you CAN use music in your podcasts but it must be specially composed original music.

There are plenty of music companies and libraries who'll licence you their own original tracks. Some are based on a specific licensing duration; others are based on a buy-out. There are composers everywhere who are eager to produce something for your podcast.

You'll be fine if you do not just copy your favourite 1990s hits onto your podcast!

Branding

It's important you pick a name for your podcast that's unique and not already taken. The first person to use a brand name has the right to use it and prevent other people from using it. You can go through a legal process to protect the name of your podcast through a trademark.

If you infringe someone's trademark, you're likely to come to the attention of the trademark holder who'll probably take action. This usually takes the form of a cease-and-desist letter demanding that you stop using the name and take down all previous references. You'll end up having no choice but to be forced into changing the name of your podcast. So, choose a podcast name that hasn't already been taken.

Ownership

Not only do you need to own your podcast, but you also need to own the artwork and other relevant elements used to promote it. Any independent contractors who create any logos or artwork should be covered by written agreements.

If you don't, you open yourself to a dispute. The written agreement with anyone who's created artwork ensures that they've transferred all rights in the artwork to you for your use.

If your podcast has co-hosts or the same people on every episode, then it's desirable to have written agreements in place to specify who owns the podcast and the various rights and responsibilities. This particularly applies if the podcast is being monetised as an agreement would indicate who gets what.

It's usually best to pay a small fee for a solicitor to draw up agreements like this as, in the long term, this could be money well spent.

What's a Release Form and When Should I Use One?

The fact that a guest agrees to appear on your podcast essentially gives you implied permission to use the interview.

To give yourself maximum flexibility in the future, you should ask your guests to agree to a release that gives you the right to use the content however you want.

Without a release, a disgruntled former guest could demand you edit their episodes in a certain way; demand payment for the continued right to distribute it; demand you remove their episode from your feed; and potentially sue you for damages.

Releases don't have to be wordy or scary. They can just be a couple of sentences. There are various templates for short and simple release forms and wording available online which can be found with a search.

The form needs to be signed before recording or production. You can even record release language at the beginning of your podcast or interview which your guest agrees to before you proceed. Obviously, you'll edit this out of the publicly distributed episode but you then have the interviewee agreeing to your release on the record.

The language you use needn't be complicated. You could say something like: "Just a quick release here. I want to ensure that I have your permission to use your name, likeness and any information you share. You understand that we're going to share it so that listeners throughout the world can hear it and we both agree that I'm the owner of all rights to this content. Is that agreed?"

The Best Advice?

If In Doubt, Leave It Out

About the Authors

PAUL CHANTLER has spent 40 years in the radio industry as a journalist, presenter, producer and programme executive. He was Group Programme Director at three of the UK's biggest radio groups in the 1990s and over the last 20 years has built a highly successful radio consultancy company with clients in the UK, Ireland, Europe and India as well as helping to start innovative new radio stations in the UK such as Fix Radio and Podcast Radio. He is co-author of the textbook Essential Radio Journalism, originally published 25 years ago. He regularly conducts training seminars for radio groups on Media Law and Compliance. Paul is a Fellow of the Radio Academy.

www.paulchantler.com

chantler@essentialmedialaw.com

@PaulChantler

PAUL HOLLINS is a successful and popular radio presenter who has been on-air in most of the major markets in the UK. He started his career at Key 103 in Manchester before working at BRMB in Birmingham, Capital FM London and Heart 106.2 in London. In 1999 he set-up the radio content and syndication company Blue Revolution which is now one of Europe's leading providers of programming and radio services. In 2018 he acquired the world's largest independently owned syndication company, Radio Express, based in Los Angeles. Paul currently presents shows for Smooth Radio.

www.bluerevolution.com

hollins@essentialmedialaw.com

@thepaulhollins

Acknowledgments

The authors would like to thank the following people and organisations who have been supportive or helpful in putting this book and its predecessors together (in alphabetical order):

Dennis Alvaro, Anita Antonio, Sally Ardis, James Brokenshire (RIP), Langley Brown (RIP), Martin Campbell, Stuart Clarkson, Steve Collins, James Cridland, Francis Currie, Jessica D'Agostin, James Daniels, John Dash, Tony Dibbin, Paul Easton, Gerry Edwards, Huw Edwards, Jack Edwards, Paul Emmines, Paul Fairburn, Richard Gaisford, Paul Gerrard, Neil Greenslade, Jamie Griffiths, Dorian Hardacre, Sim Harris, HM Courts and Tribunal Service, Tony Horne, Nick James, Peter Kerridge, Ivan Laskov, Alan Larcombe (RIP), Danny Lawrence, Mark Lee, David Lloyd, Kelvin MacKenzie, Rory McLeod, Roy Martin, John Myers (RIP), Richard Park, Jorge Paula-Rodrigues, John Pickford, Nick Pitts, Michelle Ponting, Archel Pokrovski, Keith Pringle, James Rea, Richard René, Phil Riley, Paul Robinson, Barbara Rounds, Tom Rounds, Samaritans, John Simons, Neil Stafford, Neil Sloan, Adrian Stewart, Peter Stewart, Dick Stone, Mark Story, Ashley Tabor-King, Dave Terris, Adam Tester, Louis Timpany, Ilian Valchev, James Wheldon, Writermotive.

Printed in Great Britain
by Amazon

25777861R00056